W9-DGE-004

WITHDRAWN

MOLIÈRE

from the portrait attributed to Charles Lebrun

MOLIÈRE -- Résumés

By

GEORGE L. HOLCOMB
Trinity University

and

HAROLD T. DAVIS
Trinity University

TRINITY UNIVERSITY PRESS SAN ANTONIO

Copyright © 1971 Trinity University Press
Library of Congress Catalogue Card No. 71-168524
Printed in the United States
By the Von Boeckman — Jones Co., Austin, Texas,
Bound by Universal Bookbindery, Inc., San Antonio
SBN No. 911536-39-6

To Our Wives
JESSIE and AGNES
who awaited so patiently the completing of it,
This Book is Affectionately Dedicated.

PREFACE

The idea for the publication of this collection of resumes of Moliere's plays came about as the result of a
fond recollection of a course on the subject taught by Professor Elijah Clarence Hills (1867-1932) at Colorado College and attended by Harold T. Davis, one of the authors of
this work. Professor Hills was one of the notable scholars
of his day in the field of romance languages and his presentation of Moliere left a vivid appreciation of the great-
ness of the dramatist. A number of resumes were written
as requirements in this course. Since only about half the
plays were reviewed at that time, when the project of pro-
ducing a complete work was undertaken, George L. Holcomb was persuaded to provide the remaining summaries.

Although a resume is a poor substitute for the complete play, it was felt that a work of this sort might have
a place in a world which is so busy and where so much
good literature has been produced that time does not permit one to read it all. If a few readers of these samplings
are encouraged to delve further into the reading and study
of complete works of one of the world's truly great dramatists, the time and effort spent in the preparation of this
book will have been worthwhile.

The two plays, *La Jalousie du Barbouille* and *Le Me-
decin volant,* did not appear in early editions of Moliere's
plays, and there is some question as to their authenticity.
Discovered in manuspcript form in the 18th century, they
finally found place among the author's works a hundred
years later. These short pieces, which are little more than
sketches, contain lines which appear in later plays of Moliere, but it is generally believed that they were written
down from memory by someone who saw them performed.

The authors would also like to take this opportunity to express their appreciation of the assistance of Joe W. Nicholson, Managing Editor of the Trinity Press, in getting this work into press; and also to acknowledge the valuable suggestions of Laura Barber in her editing of the manuscript and for her careful proofreading.

TABLE OF CONTENTS

TABLE OF CONTENTS

LIST OF ILLUSTRATIONS

MOLIÈRE -- RÉSUMÉS

THE LIFE AND WORKS OF MOLIERE

Molière, whose family name was Jean-Baptiste Poquelin, was born in Paris, probably in January, 1622. The
exact date of his birth is unknown, as is the exact place,
which was probably a house on the Rue Saint Honoré.
Equally obscure is the dramatist's reason for choosing
his *nom de théâtre*.

Molière's father was Jean Poquelin, an upholsterer,
who in 1631 succeeded his uncle as "valet tapissier de
chambre du roi." The family came from Beauvais, where
for centuries they had been prosperous tradesmen. The
mother of Molière, Marie Cressé, died in 1632, and his
father remarried the following year. Jean Poquelin owned
some shops in the covered Halle de la Foire, Saint Germain des Près, and it is possible that the spectacles offered to the holiday people at the fair may have had some
influence in Molière's leaning toward the stage.

Little is known of Molière's early education. His
mother possessed a Bible and a copy of Plutarch's *Lives*,
and it is reasonable to assume than an intelligent and in-
quisitive child such as young Jean-Baptiste would have
familiarized himself with these two works. At the Collège
de Clermont, where he studied until 1641, Molière probably took part in dramatic productions and in ballets. He
also studied Aristotelian philosophy. Upon leaving Clermont he became associated with Gassendi, who taught
him to appreciate the atomic philosophy of Lucretius.
These philosophical studies, which included a translation of *De rerum natura*, left a deep mark on the genius
of Molière. A favorite exercise of his was talking philosophy, and his ideas on the subject are to be found in
several of his plays.

After college Molière studied law, and there is some evidence that he may actually have been called to the bar. However, La Grange, a close friend and fellow-actor, declared that Molière went directly from law school into the theater. Meanwhile, Jean Poquelin had obtained for his son the right to succeed him as "valet tapissier de chambre du roi," and there is good reason to believe that Molière had some experience in his father's business. Part of the romance of Molière even has him as the young "valet de chambre" who concealed Cinq Mars just before the latter's arrest at Narbonne, on the 13th of June, 1642.

On January 6, 1643, Molière renounced his claim to succeed his father, and on June 30 of the same year he joined a theatrical group which included the Béjarts, near neighbors of the Poquelins in the Rue Saint Honoré. Molière's connection with this family was to bring him much unhappiness. The most noted of the many children of Joseph Béjart and his wife Marie Hervé were Joseph, Madeleine, Geneviève, and Armande. Madeleine, a talented actress, was a close friend and perhaps the mistress of Molière through all the years of his wanderings. Armande, shown in official records as still not christened in March, 1643, was to become the wife of Molière in 1662. This marriage created a scandal, for enemies of Molière attempted to show that Armande could not have been the daughter of Marie Hervé, who was fifty-three years old at the time the child was born, and that Armande was actually the child of Madeleine, with the additional implication that she might well have been Molière's own daughter. Montfleury, the famous actor of the Hôtel de Bourgogne, denounced Molière to the king, implying that he had committed a sort of incest by marrying the daughter of his former mistress. The King, Louis XIV, replied to this accusation by being himself the god-father of Molière's firstborn child, Louis, in February, 1664.

Much has been written since that time and documents have been presented on both sides of the question. Madeleine is known to have had at least one i l l e g i t i m a t e child, and the circumstances surrounding the birth of Armande are sufficiently beclouded to permit speculation, leading to the scandalous attacks on Molière which continued into the nineteenth century.

To return to the order of events, Molière spent the year 1643 playing with and helping to manage the theatrical company, which called itself L'Illustre Théâtre. The company acted in various tennis courts which were turned into theaters at no little cost to the group. Despite some outside f i n a n c i a l help and the gift of a cast-off wardrobe from one benefactor, the company was unable to draw enough customers into its makeshift theaters to meet its financial needs, and it was finally obliged to leave Paris near the end of 1645.

A number of travelling companies had found it possible to exist in the provinces, and Molière decided to try his fortune in the rural towns. Life was not easy at first for such a group. Transportation was primitive. Lumbering carts, drawn by horses and mules, were used to transport the wardrobe and other properties. Crowded and noisy inns provided temporary living accomodations. Tennis courts were quickly converted into theaters, with tapestries and curtains crudely hung around the stage. Candles provided the essential lighting effects, and two or three violins, or a flute and tambour, supplied the necessary music. Performances began at two o'clock in the afternoon.

The itinerary of Molière's company is difficult to follow. They were in Bordeaux, where it is said that Molière's failure as a tragic actor brought on a barrage of fruits and vegetables thrown by an unappreciative audience. From 1650 to 1653 the troupe made its headquarters at Lyons, where, according to La Grange, Molière's first comedy, *L'Etourdi*, was presented. It was at Lyons also that de Brie and his wife, the famous Mille de Brie, joined the troupe, and du Parc, one of the regular members, married a young "marquise" who became known as Mlle du Parc. These two women were to play an important and interesting part in the Molière tradition.

In 1653 Molière's fortunes took an upward turn when chance brought him into contact with a former Clermont schoolfellow, the famous Prince de Conti. Given the opportunity to perform for Conti in the latter's private theater near Pézenas, in Languedoc. Molière's company made such a favorable impression that they were provided with a pension and adopted as the prince's own troupe. For the next few years the group lived well while performing as the quasi-official entertainers of the government representatives in this part of France.

In 1656 Molière presented for the first time, at Béziers, his second major comedy, *Le Dépit amoureux*, It was in this year also that Conti began to "make his soul," and one of his first acts of penitence was to withdraw support for Molière's troupe. Ten years later he would write a treatise condemning his old friend, whose theater he now called a school of atheism. Meanwhile, however, Molière had made his place and was now independent of princes and their favor. In 1657 he began another circuit which took him to Nismes, Orange, Avignon, Lyons, Grenoble, and finally to Rouen, where he had played once in 1643. Here he must have made, or renewed, the acquaintance of Pierre and Thomas Corneille, whose pieces he had played at Lyons and elsewhere. It was here also that he began to plan for his return to Paris. With the help of the king's brother he was able to present his troupe for the first time before Louis XIV in a theater in the old Louvre on October 24, 1658. *Nico-*

mède, by the elder Corneille, was the piece, and the performance was all but a failure. When the play was over,
Molière asked the king's permission to perform one of the
lighter pieces that had delighted the people of the provinces. Permission was granted and the group presented a
farce, the text of which, unfortunately, has been lost. The
play, *Le Docteur amoureux,* so pleased the audience and
the king that the latter ordered the troupe to establish
itself in Paris as the "Troupe de Monsieur," and provided them with a theater called the Petit Bourbon,
which was shared by a group of Italian players. *L'Etourdi,*
the first piece played in the new house, was a brilliant
success. This was followed by the second of Molière's
major comedies, *Le Dépit amoureux,* which also pleased
the Paris audience.

On November 18, 1659, following a production of Corneille's *Cinna,* Molière presented an original short piece,
Les Précieuses ridicules, the first true comic satire of
contemporary foibles on the French stage. It was in this
play that Molière's comic genius found its first individual expression. Several of the characters in the piece
bear the names of actors in Molière's company, including La Grange, Du Croisy and Jodelet. It is probable that
the parts of Magdelon, Cathos and Marotte were played
by Madeleine Béjart, Catherine de Brie and Marie Rag8-
neau respectively. Molière himself played the role of Mascarille, as he had in *L'Etourdi.* Enemies of Molière
charged him with plagiarism and literary larceny, one of
the stock criticisms which the dramatist was to suffer
all his life. The play also raised the question as to
whether the ladies of the Hôtel de Rambouillet, or merely
their rustic imitators, were being laughed at. Molière always insisted that the latter were the butt of his jibes,
but a mysterious delay of two weeks between the prem-
ière and the second performance may have been due to

the influence of some friends of the *précieuses*. In spite
of all the attacks against him, Molière was the eventual
victor. The play was successful, the satire powerful;
nevertheless, we find him returning later in *Le Misanthrope* and *Les Femmes savantes,* to continue his attack
on what he considered the artificiality of the *précieux*
movement.

Molière's next piece, *Sganarelle ou le Cocu imaginaire,* is pure farce. A one-act play in verse, it had more
performances during the author's life than any other, and
it established him as the most popular writer of comedies
of his day. The series of logical and understandable misunderstandings arising from a succession of improbable
situations is handled in a happy manner. The public liked
the play, and it is said that the king himself was pleased
to witness it on no less than nine occasions. A few
months after the appearance of this play, the theater being used by Molière's company was suddenly and without
warning razed by order of the official in charge of building operations at the Louvre. The king gave the group a
new location, but the machinery of the old theater was
destroyed, and for a time the company played in the
houses of the great and before the king at the Louvre.
During the time the new theater, the Palais-Royal, was
being put in order, Molière's rivals in the older companies of the Hôtel de Bourgogne and the Théâtre du Marais
tried unsuccessfully to lure away members of his troupe.

On January 20, 1661, Molière began to play in the
new house, and on February 4th he presented *Dom Garcie
de Navarre,* his only tragedy. The play failed, and oppo-
nents quickly and eagerly seized upon his failure as an
opportunity to attack him and fortify their claim that his
talents were limited to farce and comedy. We must admire
Molière's obstinate devotion to the tragic muse in the
face of repeated failures.

Molière was now contemplating marriage, and he asked for two shares in the profits of his company. one for himself, and one for his wife, in case he should marry. Before taking that fatal step he brought out two new plays. The first of these, *L'Ecole des maris,* resulted in new charges of larceny and pilfering, for the theme goes back to Menander and Terence, and parts of the story seem to have been lifted right out of Boccaccio. In this play, which may be a reflection of Molière's concern for his own plans to marry a young, spoiled woman half his age, two opposing conceptions of the education of young women for marriage are presented, and judgment is given in favor of freedom and a reasonable indulgence.

The second new piece, *Les Fâcheux,* a *comédie-ballet,* was played before the king at a reception given by Fouquet, the king's rival for the affection of La Vallière. The fundamental idea of the play, a series of interruptions by bores, goes back to a satire by Horace. Some of the apparently innocuous scenes reflect in reality some of the intrigues and schemes being engaged in at the time, including those of Fouquet and the king, and each bore could be matched with an original in the brilliant audience. After the performance the king drew the author's attention to another famous bore, his own Master of the Chase, and in a subsequent revival Molière included a Sportsman among the group of tedious and discocerting meddlers whose inopportune appearances delay a young lover in his efforts to reach a rendezvous with his sweetheart.

As mentioned earlier, the marriage with Armande Béjart took place in February, 1662. The questionable conduct of his young wife brought further troubles to an already harassed Molière, as his enemies accused her of all kinds of improprieties and labeled him a cuckold. Molière himself never admitted that he had ever been deceived by his wife, but he did confess to extreme jealousy, which he nevertheless m a i n t a i n e d was without foundation. Charges against Mlle Molière are unsubstantiated, and it is generally thought that Molière is describing her when he says of Lucile in *Le Bourgeois gentilhomme* that "she is capricious but one endures anything from beautiful women." The fundamental incompatibility between them is later i d e a l i z e d in the encounters between Alceste and Célimène in *Le Misanthrope*. There were long periods of separation during which they saw each other only at the theater. She bore him three children, two sons and a daughter. The first son, the god-son of the king, died at the age of about nine months. The daughter, born in 1665, died in 1723, leaving no descendants. The second son, born in 1672, lived for only a few days.

Rival actors continued to plague Molière, some of them even appealing to the queen mother in an attempt to obtain special favors. On December 26, 1662, he presented *L'Ecole des femmes*, provoking a veritable literary war as well as charges of indecency and irreverence. An excellent study of male jealousy, the play pictures in the character of Arnolphe a middle-aged man infatuated with a young woman of whom he could never be sure. Some have seen this as a reflection of the concerns of the author himself after ten months of marriage to just such a woman.

Against the initial literary attacks Molière replied with his own *Critique de l'école des femmes*, a piece in which he attacked his most f o r m i d a b l e critics and which he succeeded in d e d i c a t i n g to the very devout queen mother. The assaults continued and Molière again countered with his *L'Impromptu de Versailles*, a merciless and witty attack on his critics, one of the foremost of whom, Boursault, was mentioned by name. The latter

had printed a play, *Portrait du peintre,* in which the characters had described Molière's *L'Ecole des femmes,* as
dull, vulgar, farcical, obscene and impious. This last
accusation was, of course, a serious and dangerous one
and had to be answered. Molière's play also ridiculed the
art of the actors of the rival company, the Hôtel de Bourgogne. Several more major attacks and defenses were written in the following months as the original play continued
to run. Although the attacks were based primarily on alleged impieties, there is no doubt that Molière's contemporaries were profoundly disconcerted by the latter's lib-
eral views on the freedom of women and the confidence
which should be placed in their discretion.

Molière decided that the best way to answer his enemies was to produce another successful comedy, and on
January 29, 1664, in the apartments of the queen mother
he presented a hastily written prose *comédie-ballet* called
Le Mariage forcé. Louis XIV himself danced in the ballet
as an Egyptian. Although the play was an improvement
over *Les Fâcheux,* his first attempt at this genre, it was
not a brilliant success. The story is that of an old man
who has decided to get married for the first time and who,
like Panurge in the novel by Rabelais, asks the advice
of a number of people, among them two philosophers of
different schools. This gives Molière an opportunity to
discuss one of his favorite subjects, philosophy.

On May 8, 1664, during a magnificent festival staged
at Versailles, Molière presented a new *comédie-ballet,*
called *La Princesse d'Elide,* the model for which may
have been a play by the Spanish dramatist Moreto, called
El desdén con el desdén. The scene is Greece, the occasion is a festival such as that being celebrated by Louis
XIV, and the story is that of a prince who wins the heart
and hand of a disdainful princess by pretending to be
even more disdainful than she. Molière played the part of

the buffoon, and when the play was later presented in Paris, it had a long and successful run.

In addition to *La Princesse*, Molière presented two of his other plays, *Les Fâcheux* and *Le Mariage forcé*, during the week-long festival. The most significant event of the entire occasion, however, as far as Molière and the French theater were concerned, was the first performance of a version of *Tartuffe* in three acts. This production was the beginning of an even more violent battle between Molière and his enemies than that occasioned by *L'Ecole des femmes*. A vicious attack on religious bigotry and hypocricy, the play made enemies everywhere, and it was not until February 5, 1669, that a public performance of the play, in its final form and under its proper title, was finally authorized. During this period of almost five years, the king had been forced to intervene on more than one occasion, and Molière had threatened to retire from the theater.

The charges of blasphemy brought on after the *Ecole des femmes* had only increased Molière's natural hatred of hypocrisy. Fighting fire with fire, he returned to the attack on February 15, 1665, with his *Don Juan ou le Festin de Pierre*. In this play Molière went further than any of those who had treated previously the familiar legend of Don Juan. The hero of this version is an evil man, and religion seems to have been replaced by what is called "l'humanité." The play was considered not only blasphemous and irreligious, but also a deliberate attack on the nobility. Again the king came to the defense of Molière, granting him and his company a pension and adopting them as his own "Troupe du roi."

The first play Molière presented as head of the king's company brought him further enemies, this time from the medical profession. *L'Amour médecin*, a *comédie-ballet* written and staged in five days, was first presented at Versailles on September 15, 1665. In this satire of the medical profession in general, Molière caricatures four doctors, contemporaries of the author, who typify the pretentiousness, the pedantry, the cult of ancient authority, and the impotence of the practitioners of the times. There is nothing new in the theme that doctors are more harmful than helpful in the treatment of the sick. Molière himself had touched on the matter in an earlier farce, and his final work was to be an attack on this profession, most of the members of which did not even accept the fact of the circulation of the blood.

For two years Molière had been encouraging a rising young dramatist named Racine and had produced two of his plays. In December, 1665, Racine, suddenly and without notifying Molière, took the second play and gave it to a rival company, the Hôtel de Bourgogne. Molière took this as an affront to his actors and a betrayal of his friendship, and the brief association between the two greatest dramatists of the period was at an end. Shortly thereafter Molière became seriously ill, and his theater was closed for several weeks. Finally, on June 4, 1666, he presented what is perhaps his finest comedy, *Le misanthrope*. The general public, as well as the court, found the play too subtle for its tastes, but later generations have come to admire it as one of the author's best. The part of the inflexible Alceste was played by Molière and that of the frivolous Célimène by his wife. The conflict is between virtue and convenience, between the just man and a society based on compromise. The play produced no great controversy in Molière's time, but in the eighteenth century Rousseau attacked the work as immoral and vicious, since virtue in Alceste is made ridiculous, and vice is praised in the person of Philinte. This criticism is not necessarily justified, since the ideal man of the seventeenth century, the *honnête homme*, cannot be an extremist like Alceste, but must be well rounded and follow a middle course.

On August 6, 1666, Molière presented *Le Médecin malgré lui,* an amusing farce based on an old "fabliau." Some of the scenes may have been inspired by Rabelais' story of the man who had his wife cured of her dumbness, only to regret his action later when he could not stop her from talking. The success of the play was immediate, and it has never lost its popularity. Another maltreatment of the medical profession, Molière's play has as its theme the revenge which a wife takes on her husband by telling others that the only way they can persuade him to admit that he is a great physician is to beat him severely.

From December 1, 1666, to February 20, 1667, Saint Germain was the scene of another of those grand festivals of which the king was so fond. Molière contributed three items to the event: *Mélicerte, La Pastorale Comique,* and *Le Sicilien.* The first of these is a pastoral based on a tale from Mlle de Scudéry's *Le Grand Cyrus.* The second, a ballet, is a burlesque of the genre and, incidentally, of one of the famous bassos of the period. *Le Sicilien* is a charming little piece which had a successful run later in Paris.

Molière's health was now a matter of concern, and the fact that he was getting little relief from the doctors who attended him did not lessen his antagonism toward a profession which he considered pedantic and antiquated. The battle over *Tartuffe* was continuing, and relations with his wife were at their worst. He left Paris to stay with his friend Chapelle at the latter's villa at Auteuil. There he was visited by a few of his faithful friends, including Boileau and La Fontaine. In January, 1668, he returned to the theater with a new type of play, an adaptation of the *Amphytrion* of Plautus. Completely modernized, the story is no longer a tragedy, and it contains many gay and farcical scenes. Many saw in it an attempt to ridicule the husband of the king's new mistress.

For a summer festival at Versailles, Molière wrote *George Dandin,* a satiric comedy which Molière played successfully as a farce. The name Dandin is borrowed from Rabelais, the story is from Boccaccio and from the author's own observation of contemporary French society, where the type of George Dandin was well known. On September 9, 1668, Molière presented in Paris another of his truly great plays, *L'Avare.* Apparently he had spent the past year at Auteuil re-reading the classics, for this is another borrowing from Plautus. Although it was coolly received by the French audience, the play has become one of the most popular of Molière's comedies. Actors vie for the chance to play the role of Harpagon, which the author himself created in the original production.

A farce, *M. de Pourceaugnac,* was first acted before the king at Chamborg in October of 1669, and was another in a series of attacks on the medical profession. *Les Amants magnifiques,* a *comédie-ballet* first presented at Saint Germain in February 1670, is a satire on astrology. In October of this year the king was again at Chamborg enjoying the hunting season. He called for Molière, and the latter had one of his greatest successes there with *Le Bourgeois gentilhomme.* Turks were very much in fashion at the moment, and the Turkish ballet was a big hit with the king and with the audiences. Molière played the role of Monsieur Jourdain in this original play of a bourgeois social climber.

The constant demands being placed on Molière by the king were taking their toll. A new spectacle, commanded for the Tuileries in the following January was a *Tragédie-ballet* on the theme of *Psyche.* The play, often referred to as an opera, was elaborately staged, with twelve violins, a large group of singers, and three hundred dancers.

Music was by the best composers of the day, and Pierre
Corneille collaborated on the dialogue. On May 24, 1671,
the first performance of *Les Fourberies de Scapin* was
given at the Palais-Royal. For this play Molière borrowed
from a number of sources, including Plautus and Terence,
and came up with a mixture of Italian comedy and French
farce. The play did not enjoy much success in the life-
time of the author, but the role of Scapin has always been
a favorite of the great comic actors.

Summoned again by the king, this time to prepare a
celebration for the second marriage of the latter's brother,
Molière improvised a ballet from previous productions,
and wrote a little comedy, *La Comtesse d'Escarbagnas,*
with which to begin the spectacle. This is a delightful
study of provincial manners in which, among other things,
Molière attacks the financiers of the times.

On February 17, 1672 Madeleine Béjart died, and it
may be said that part of Molière died with her, for he was
to survive her by only a year. On March 11 *Les Femmes
savantes* had its first performance at the Palais-Royal.
Molière had worked for four years on this play, which is
an attack on the foibles of contemporary society. It may
be said to be an extension of *Les Précieuses ridicules,*
with some added pretentions and with models taken from
the local scene. Molière's health was rapidly deteriorat-
ing. He suffered a formidable blow when the king granted
to the musician Lully a monopoly in music and ballet.
On October 11 his second son died, adding to his sor-
rows.

On February 10, 1673, *Le Malade imaginaire* was presented for the first time, with Molière in the title role.
During a performance a week later he was seized with a
violent coughing spell which apparently caused a blood
vessel to burst. He finished the performance, after which
he was taken home and put to bed. A few hours later he

was dead, a victim of the old adage, "the show must go on." As a member of the acting profession Molière was denied the final rites of the Catholic church and consequently the right to a proper Christian burial. When his wife appealed to the king, only a compromise resulted from this final intervention of a friend on behalf of a faithful servant. There was no ceremony at the burial, which occurred after sunset, and there is even doubt that the priests allowed him to be buried, as the king had directed, in consecrated ground, for, when an attempt was made to exhume the body in 1792, the wrong tomb appears to have been opened. The resting place of France's greatest literary figure is unknown to this day.

Four years after her husband's death, Armande remarried. Meanwhile, in May, 1673, La Grange, fellow-actor and for years the right hand of Molière in the management of the troupe, arranged a merger of the company with an old rival, the Théâtre du Marais. A month later this company joined a group called the Hôtel de Guénégaud. In 1680, by order of the king, the Hôtel de Guénégaud, also referred to as the "ancienne troupe de Molière," joined with the Hôtel de Bourgogne to form the Comédie-Française, with La Grange as its head, or "doyen." Today the company which has been France's principal theatrical group for almost three centuries lists Molière as its first "doyen" and the year 1658 as the date of its beginning, this despite the fact that the Hôtel de Bourgogne dates back to 1548 and is itself the descendant of a group formed in 1402. In 1682 La Grange published, with Vinot, the first complete edition of the works of Molière. In the preface to the eight-volume work, he included a brief, but excellent, biography of the dramatist.

Molière has been described as neither too stout nor too thin, tall rather than short, of noble carriage and

serious e x p r e s s i o n, with eyes that seemed to search
the depths of men's hearts. He was fond of rich dress,
splendid furniture and old books. The fact that he counted
among his friends the greatest wits of his day attests to
the charm of his conversation. As an actor he was at his
best in comedy, for his tragic style was ahead of his time.
In private he was gentle, honest and generous. His sense
of the true value of life, coupled with a vivacious wit
and acute powers of observation combined to make him
perhaps the greatest of all writers of social and refined
comedy. His plays are still much alive today, many of
them forming part of the repertory of major theatrical com=
panies. They delight, if possible, even more in the per=
formance than in the reading.

THE BLUNDERER

THE BLUNDERER

(L'ETOURDI)

CHARACTERS IN THE PLAY

LELIE: son of Pandolfe.

CELIE: slave girl, in pawn to Trufaldin.

MASCARILLE: servant of Lelie.

HIPPOLYTE: daughter of Anselme.

ANSELME: an old man.

TRUFALDIN: an old man.

PANDOLFE: father of Lelie.

LEANDRE: a young gentleman.

ANDRES: a young gentleman dressed as a gypsy.

ERGASTE: friend of Mascarille.

POSTMAN

TWO MASKED COMPANIES

The Scene is a Public Place in Messina.

ACT I.

Lelie and Leandre are rivals for the love of Celie, a slave girl belonging to Trufaldin. Lelie's father Pandolfe has promised Anselme that Lelie will marry the latter's daughter Hippolyte. A solution to Lelie's predicament is suggested by his servant, Mascarille. Mascarille advises that Lelie purchase the slave girl. First, however, Lelie must talk with Celie and determine her feelings on the matter. He fumbles his chance by wasting time with fancy words, and Trufaldin interrupts, reminding Celie that she is not to speak to anyone. Lelie retires into a corner, and Mascarille takes over. Celie, pretending to be skilled in fortune-telling and speaking of the parties concerned as though they were others, makes it clear to Mascarille that Lelie's hopes are not in vain. At this moment Lelie approaches and spoils everything by offering to purchase the girl. Trufaldin recognizes the scheme and removes himself and Celie from the scene.

Mascarille, promising to help Anselme in a love affair, so distracts the old man that the latter does not notice that the wily servant has removed his purse and placed it on the ground nearby. At this moment Lelie approaches and points out the purse to Anselme, thereby spoiling Mascarille's plan to get the money with which to purchase the slave girl.

Pretending to have quarreled with Lelie and to be on the side of Pandolfe, Mascarille suggests that the latter ask Anselme to purchase Celie from Trufaldin and turn her over to Mascarille. Mascarille will then sell her to some merchant acquaintances, and Pandolfe can proceed with his plan to marry Lelie to Hippolyte.

Hippolyte, who is in love with Leandre, has overheard the conversation and accuses Mascarille of treachery in failing to keep his promise to help her in her plan to marry Leandre. Mascarille explains that the scheme is one in which Celie is to be turned over to Lelie, thereby forcing Anselme to accept Leandre as his son-in-law. Mascarille pretends to be hurt by her false accusations and threatens to halt the entire scheme. Desperate, Hippolyte heals Mascarille's wounds with a nice gift of money.

Lelie arrives to announce that he has just prevented Anselme from purchasing Celie from Trufaldin and carrying her off. Mascarille explains that another well-laid plan, his third, has just been spoiled by Lelie's blundering.

ACT II.

Mascarille's next scheme involves, among other things, letting the word out that Pandolfe has died suddenly of apoplexy. Lelie is let in on the plan in the hope that his clumsiness will not spoil this one. Mascarille convinces Anselme that Pandolfe must be buried immediately so that Lelie's sorrow will not increase to the extent that he might commit suicide. In addition Anselme agrees to lend Lelie the money necessary for a splendid funeral for his father.

Lelie feigns great sorrow as Anselme tries to console him, and he can only repeat "Oh" in response to all of Anselme's remarks, including the offer of money. He leaves without signing a note, a small matter which Mascarille promises to take care of. At this moment Pandolfe appears, and Alselme reacts as though he is seeing a ghost. Pandolfe thinks that Anselme is joking, and he goes along with it for a time. But then Pandolfe, puzzling over Anselme's continued reference to the former as a ghost, concludes finally that he and Anselme have been made the victims of another of Mascarille's tricks. The ruse becomes clear as the two friends talk. First of all Pandolphe was lured out of the city by a false story that treasure had been discovered on his country property. Then the tale was spread in the city that Pandolfe was dead so that Lelie and Mascarille could obtain money from Anselme, supposedly to be used for Pandolfe's funeral expenses.

Finding Lelie, Anselme pretends that some of the coins he has just given him are counterfeit and he wishes to replace them with good ones. In this way he succeeds in recovering his money, and at the same time he dismisses Lelie forever as a candidate for Celie's hand.

Mascarille arrives, ready to carry out his scheme to purchase Celie, only to find that Lelie has blundered again. Threatening to stop helping such an imprudent fellow, he appears not to be moved by Lelie's threats of suicide. Suddenly they see Leandre in the act of purchasing Celie from Trufaldin. Lelie leaves quickly, and Mascarille puts another plan into action. Complaining that he has been beaten for no reason at all by Lelie, he hurries to tell Leandre that he would like nothing better than to get revenge on his master. Leandre, taken in by the ruse and anxious to avoid the responsibility of taking care of the slave girl at the moment, willingly turns over to Mascarille a ring which will identify him as the person to whom Celie is to be delivered. Mascarille's plan is to lodge the girl at the home of a relative in the country.

At this moment Hippolyte arrives and leads Leandre toward the church. Meanwhile, Mascarille finds Trufaldin and is about to receive his prize, when a postman approaches with a letter for Trufaldin. The message is from a Don Pedro de Gusman stating that Celie is his daughter, stolen from him years before by a band of robbers, that he is coming for her soon, and that he will reward handsomely her present owner. Trufaldin, understandably, refuses to turn the girl over to Mascarille, and he leaves the disappointed servant to ponder again a well-laid plan gone awry. Meanwhile, Lelie, gloating over the success

of his latest trick, arrives to explain that he is the author
of the fictitious letter.

ACT III.

Discouraged by the bumbling efforts of his master,
Mascarille nevertheless refuses to give up. His honor and
his reputation as a clever servant are at stake, and he
must try once more. Leandre has learned that the letter
was a trick, and he is determined to marry Celie. Mascarille, however, easily convinces him that Celie is not the
innocent, virtuous girl he thinks she is, and it appears
that a minor skirmish has been won for Lelie. However,
when Leandre explains to Lelie that he has just learned
from Mascarille that Celie is a woman of easy virtue and
that he is no longer interested in her, Lelie defends her
vigorously, and the two rivals seek out Mascarille to have
a showdown on the matter. Mascarille tries to explain to
Lelie in a whisper that the slander is a contrived story,
but Lelie, blinded by passion and fury, refuses to understand, and he draws his sword to punish his unworthy servant. Leandre then reveals that Mascarille is working for
him, and out of the confusion which results from this revelation, Leandre realizes that the alleged beating by Lelie
was just another stratagem of Mascarille to defeat him in
his efforts to obtain Celie. Lelie has blundered again. He
insists that his blundering results from ignorance of what
Mascarille plans to do each time, but the latter flatly
states that his master is, and always will be, a simple ass
in these matters.

Mascarille insists, as the next move, that Lelie make
peace with his father and agree to his demands. Otherwise
a suit filed against Mascarille as the result of the false
death notice might land that unfortunate person in jail and
deprive Lelie of his services. Lelie agrees, and as he

leaves, Mascarille learns from his friend Ergaste that
Leandre, taking advantage of a local custom which permits
women to don masks and pay visits in the evenings to
homes in the neighborhood, plans to enter Trufaldin's
house tonight and carry off Celie. Mascarille decides to
get there first with his own company disguised as women,
carry off Celie, and leave Leandre to be accused of the
crime. Meanwhile, Ergaste has revealed Leandre's plan
to Lelie, who hastens to warn Trufaldin. When Mascarille
and his company arrive, Lelie, expecting to discover his
rival, unmasks his faithful and long-suffering servant,
spoiling yet another well-laid plan in his behalf. When
Leandre's company arrives later, Trufaldin, alerted, refuses them entrance.

ACT IV.

Trufaldin, who has been convinced that Mascarille is
on his side, tells the servant of his past life. Formerly
known as Zanobio Ruberti, Trufaldin lived in Naples with
his wife and children until he was forced to leave the city
and his family because of an accusation brought against
him. He heard later that his wife and daughter had died
and his son Horace, together with the boy's tutor Albert,
had disappeared from Bolognia where they were living.
It has been twelve years since Trufaldin has heard news of
his son or the tutor, and he assumes them to be dead. Upon hearing this tale, Mascarille decides to use it in a new
scheme to help his master. In the plan Lelie is to pose as
an Armenian merchant who has seen both Horace and Albert in Turkey. He has provided them with money with
which to redeem themselves from their condition of slavery and preceded them, charged with paying a visit to
Horace's father here. After several rehearsals of his part,
Lelie, elated over the idea of being in the same house with

his adored, accompanies Mascarille to Trufaldin's place disguised as the Armenian merchant.

Lelie becomes confused many times in trying to answer Trufaldin's questions about his son and the tutor. Mascarille rescues him as best he can each time with explanations and clarifications and helps him to avoid pitfalls by means of sly promptings. Finally Mascarille succeeds in cutting short the conversation and getting invited in for refreshments.

In a short scene in front of Trufaldin's house, Anselme lectures Leandre on his conduct of the night before, reminding him that pleasures of the flesh are shortlived, and that the husband of a woman such as Hippolyte must be above reproach. Leandre is repentant and agrees that Anselme is right.

The door of Trufaldin's house opens, and we hear Mascarille reprimanding Lelie for his absurd conduct at table with Celie. Trufaldin appears and asks for a few words alone with Mascarille. Once Lelie has gone into the house Trufaldin tells the servant that he is going to beat Lelie for being a cheat and a masquerader and later to punish Mascarille as his accomplice. He has learned Lelie's true identity from a goddaughter, Jenny, who overheard Lelie confess to Celie that he had come disguised in this manner only to be able to see her. Mascarille denies any part in the ruse, and Trufaldin requires him to prove this by assisting him in beating Lelie. The two proceed to beat the uncomprehending Lelie, and to drive him off. When Trufaldin and Mascarille reenter the house, Lelie returns and talks to Mascarille through a window. The latter explains how Lelie has blundered again by permitting the girl to overhear his remarks, and he exacts from Lelie a promise of no revenge for the beating in exchange for his continued help.

Ergaste arrives to reveal to Mascarille that a young

and noble-appearing gypsy, accompanied by an old woman, is planning to purchase Celie from her owner. Mascarille will attempt to get rid of this new threat to his master's plans by having some of his greedy friends among the officers of justice charge the young gypsy with a recently committed, unsolved robbery.

ACT V.

Lelie has blundered again. Impressed by the appearance of the young gypsy gentleman, he has taken it upon himself to vouch for this stranger and has dispersed his would-be captors. In spite of this bad news, Mascarille is determined to try again. Meanwhile, Andres, the young gypsy, has taken possession of Celie and wishes to take her away immediately. Celie feigns a violent headache and requests a delay of three or four days.

Mascarille, disguised as a Swiss, and speaking with an accent, presents himself as the owner of a furnished house where Celie may stay. It is a house belonging to Lelie's father. As Andres leaves to go for the baggage, he runs into Lelie, who reveals that this must be a scheme of his servant to get possession of a young gypsy girl for him. Alerted to Lelie's designs, Andres returns to the house and observes as Lelie unmasks Mascarille. Noting that the servant has served his master well, Andres leaves, and Lelie thinks he has finally succeeded in doing something right. However, Andres returns with Celie and informs Lelie that it would break his heart to lose her and that they will go away immediately.

Lelie realizes that he has blundered again, and he is disgusted with himself. Mascarille again refuses to give up. After learning from Celie that she feels that she must, out of gratitude, go with Andres, Mascarille determines to leave no stone unturned to remedy this situation and help his master.

Hippolyte complains to Celie that the latter has stolen the heart of both her lovers, Leandre and Lelie. Hippolyte is now on her way to try to regain Leandre.

Mascarille arrives to relate to Celie a scene which he has just witnessed. Two old women were fighting in the street. After they were separated, one of them recognized Trufaldin as Zanobio Ruberti, the father of a daughter left in her care in Naples years before. The other woman had stolen the girl, resulting in the death of the mother and the public announcement that both had died. Andres has recognized Trufaldin and has revealed himself to be the latter's son Horace. The gypsy woman has confessed that Celie is Trufaldin's daughter and hence the sister of Andres. Trufaldin and Pandolfe have agreed to the marriage of Celie and Lelie, and Pandolfe has proposed his own daughter as a wife for the newfound Horace.

Leandre asks Hippolyte's forgiveness and will marry her. Lelie, when told of his good fortune, embraces Mascarille so tightly that the latter expresses fear for Celie if he should clasp her with so much eagerness. Leandre's father will be sent for to help celebrate the joyful occasion. When Mascarille says that he feels an itch to be married, Anselme indicates that he can provide a suitable woman for him. Mascarille ends the play with the hope that "Heaven will give us children, of whom we are the fathers."

THE AMOROUS QUARREL

THE AMOROUS QUARREL
(DEPIT AMOUREUX)

CHARACTERS IN THE PLAY

ERASTE: in love with Lucile.

ALBERT: father of Lucile and of Ascagne.

GROS-RENE: valet of Eraste.

VALERE: son of Polydore.

LUCILE: daughter of Albert.

MARINETTE: maid of Lucile.

POLYDORE: father of Valere.

FROSINE: confidante of Ascagne.

ASCAGNE: daughter of Albert, but dressed as a man.

MASCARILLE: valet of Valere.

METAPHRASTE: pedant.

LA RAPIERE: bully.

The Scene is in Paris.

ACT I.

Eraste and Valere are rivals for the hand of Lucile,
who shows an obvious preference for Eraste. Valere con-
fuses Eraste by acting smug and free of jealousy in spite
of Lucile's preference for his rival. Paralleling this contest between Eraste and Valere is the one between Gros-
Rene and Mascarille, valets of the principals, for the
hand of Lucile's maid, Marinette.

Marinette brings Eraste a letter from Lucile in which
it is clear that Eraste is the favorite. However, when Valere is shown the letter, he seems unimpressed, assuring
Eraste that his own affair with Lucile is going fine, and
that she does everything for his passion that he could wish
her to. Eraste and Gros-Rene are p u z z l e d as Valere,
laughing and confident, bids them good-bye.

Mascarille arrives and adds to the mystery by revealing that Valere and Lucile are secretly married, and that
he, "two other people," and "the night" were the only
witnesses to the marriage. Understandably confused by
the vagueness of such a revelation, Eraste threatens bodily harm to Mascarille if he does not say whether or not
Lucile is in effect the wife of Valere. Mascarille will say
only that the knot was joined after five nocturnal visits,
and he invites Gros-Rene to come along with him some
night to see for himself.

Marinette returns with another letter from Lucile,
along with the request that Eraste meet her in the garden
that evening. Furious, Eraste refuses to agree to the tryst,
tears up the letter in anger, and leaves the scene. In a
parallel action, Gros-Rene shows disdain for Marinette
and walks away, leaving the latter wondering why such
favors are so ill received.

ACT II.

The second act opens with a scene between Ascagne and Frosine in which we learn that the former, although dressed in men's clothing and posing as the son of Albert, is really a girl. The deception was begun by the child's mother during a lengthy absence of the father, and has continued now for several years following the sudden death of the mother. Back of it all is a considerable legacy left to a male child, presumably the son of Albert and his wife. Later we are to learn that this male child was taken into the family in exchange for a female born to the couple about the same time and that when the male child died soon afterward, it was replaced by a female, now called by the name of the male child, Ascagne, and really the daughter originally traded for the male child.

The surprise in this scene is the revelation that Ascagne is in love with Valere, and that she is in reality the woman with whom Valere is trysting at night. Valere thinks it is Lucile, and by day he knows Ascagne as the brother of Lucile.

Lucile, apparently rejected by Eraste, decides to turn her attention to Valere, but Ascagne, understandably now, opposes this. As a brother, presumably working in the best interests of a sister under his protection, he asks Lucile not to take Valere away from "a young woman who deeply loves him." Lucile, determined to avenge the affront suffered at the hands of Eraste, plans with Marinette her course of action.

Albert is concerned about the strange manner in which Ascagne is acting recently. Fearful of losing his "son," and with him the legacy, he consults a pompous pedant, Metaphraste, whose constant interruptions and Latin and Greek quotes confuse Albert and prevent him from ever

getting to the point which he wishes to discuss. Finally, in
disgust and desperation, he drives the pedant away.

ACT III.

In the third act Mascarille calls on Albert to tell him
that Polydore wishes to discuss with him a secret which
he has discovered and which concerns both of them. Albert
thinks that the secret is that of the identity of Ascagne,
since it is Polydore and his family who have been cheated
out of an inheritance by the fraud perpetrated by Albert
and his wife. However, after the usual misunderstandings,
Albert realizes that Polydore has come to apologize for
Valere's having seduced Lucile, and to arrange for their
marriage. Albert, confused and relieved, leaves to think
it over. Valere arrives only to receive a reprimand for
his actions. He then tricks Mascarille into confessing that
he had let word of the meetings reach Polydore, but the
servant defends his action as being in the best interest of
his master. Meanwhile Albert has asked Lucile about the
matter, and of course she has denied the story. He then
confronts Valere and Mascarille with his findings. They
insist on a meeting with Lucile. Lucile is insulted by the
accusations, denies everything, refuses to listen to Mascarille's efforts to get her to confess that she has given
herself to a lover, and boxes Mascarille on the ear as she
leaves. In a clever short scene at this point, both Albert
and Valere issue dire threats to Mascarille, who cannot
understand why he is being condemned for another's sin.

ACT IV.

Ascagne and Frosine are fearful that further investiga-
tion of the supposed meetings between Valere and Lucile
will reveal the true identity of Ascagne. This will mean the

loss of wealth for Albert, and the certain loss of interest on the part of Valere in a wife without family or fortune. The two retire from the scene in order to avoid a meeting with Eraste and Gros-Rene. The latter is reporting the fruitless result of his latest effort to arrange a meeting between Eraste and Lucile. Eraste decides to punish her disdain by "cherishing a new passion in his heart," and Gros-Rene parallels this action by declaring his intention to renounce all women. There follows a long dissertation on women, with the final conclusion that woman is worse than the devil.

The next scene is one in which Eraste and Lucile, supported and seconded by their servants, go through a complete lovers' breakup, including the returning of all presents received. Then they become sentimental, argue about responsibility for the breakup, and end up by being reconciled. As the two lovers walk away together, the servants, in a parallel scene, go through a similar process, which terminates in a handshake.

ACT V.

The last act opens with a long soliloquy in which Mascarille describes himself as a typical servant, worldly and cowardly. His master, Valere, has commissioned him to obtain arms and to prepare for a showdown — which may result in an armed battle — in Lucile's chamber tonight.

Valere, the typical romantic lover, yearns for night to come so that he can carry out his plan. Mascarille feigns a cough in a futile attempt to get out of the escapade. Valere rejects an offer of aid from La Rapiere, a strong-arm type who warns him of the danger he faces.

In a scene between Ascagne and Frosine, the latter explains that she has revealed to both Albert and Polydore proof of the real identity of Ascagne, and that Polydore is not only willing but anxious to see her married to Valere. Polydore arrives, sends Ascagne to fetch her people, and then brings in Valere and Mascarille for a meeting of the principals. Polydore has his little joke, however, declaring that Valere's greatest enemy is to be Ascagne, still thought by Valere to be the brother of Lucile, and that the latter is to be married to Eraste before his very eyes.

Albert, Lucile and Eraste arrive, followed by Ascagne, who pretends to wish to do battle with Valere for the honor of the family. After some amusement at Valere's fury, Polydore reveals that it has been Ascagne — real name Dorothee — whom Valere has been seeing. Valere gladly accepts Dorothee, apologizes to Lucile for the trouble he has caused her, and Dorothee leaves to change into woman's clothes.

Mascarille willingly cedes Marinette to Gros-Rene, with the warning that their marriage will not prevent her receiving gallants after their wedding.

The Prince of Conti
by M. Polly.

THE PRETENTIOUS YOUNG LADIES

THE PRETENTIOUS YOUNG LADIES

(LES PRECIEUSES RIDICULES)

CHARACTERS IN THE PLAY

LA GRANGE AND DU CROISY: rejected suitors.

GORGIBUS: father of Magdelon and uncle of Cathos.

MAGDELON AND CATHOS: pretentious young ladies.

MAROTTE: maid to Magdelon and Cathos.

ALMANZOR: footman to Magdelon and Cathos.

THE MARQUIS DE MASCARILLE: La Grange's valet.

THE VISCOUNT JODELET: Du Croisy's valet.

TWO CHAIRMEN

CELIMENE AND LUCILE: neighbor women.

MUSICIANS

The Scene is in Paris at the home of Gorgibus.

The play opens with Du Croisy and La Grange planning revenge on Magdelon and Cathos, two young women who have rejected them because their courting manners and their dress are not in the latest fashion. As the two young noblemen discuss their plan, Gorgibus interrupts and inquires as to the success of their visit. Sensing that all is not well, he calls the two girls in to find out what they have done to discourage their suitors. They explain to the confused Gorgibus that a proposal of marriage must, according to the current rules of courtship, be preceded by certain "adventures," and that the suitor must dress extravagantly. Gorgibus, who is responsible for the two girls, threatens to put them in a convent if they do not marry soon.

As the two girls ponder over the lack of understanding on the part of Gorgibus, Marotte announces the arrival of the Marquis de Mascarille, transported by two chairmen. The Marquis is in reality La Grange's valet, extraordinary wit and imitator, who prides himself on his gallantry and his poetry. He is the tool of vengeance sent by the rejected suitors to make fools of the country wenches, with their newly acquired affectation.

Mascarille tells the young ladies that their reputation has brought him to pay them a visit. He charms them with his elegant speech, manners and dress, and he promises to establish an academy of wits in their house where poets will gather to recite their poems. He also promises to show them some of his portraits, and he regales them with some extempore verses composed by him the day before at the home of a duchess. All admire the brilliance and the wit of the madrigal, commenting on it phrase by phrase. Mascarille then offers to sing the madrigal to a tune which he has written for it. When Cathos wonders how one who has never studied music can compose a tune, Mascarille replies that people of rank know everything

without ever having learned anything. His singing further
charms the girls and, in response to their compliments,
he assures them that all he does comes naturally and
without study.

Mascarille then promises to take the girls to the performance of a play which the author recently has read to
him for his approval and support. This leads to a modest
admission that he too has written a play, which he plans
to offer to the actors of the theatrical group known as the
Hotel de Bourgogne.

Conversation now turns to dress, with appropriate
comments on the elegance of the ornaments and the deli-
cate odors of certain items which Mascarille is wearing.
Marotte interrupts to announce the arrival of Viscount
Jodelet, who is in reality Du Croisy's valet. The mas-
querade and the game of vengeance continue. The Viscount
is presented as an old friend of Mascarille. The two rem-
inisce about their exploits in battle, and they show the
girls scars from wounds received in various campaigns.

Mascarille asks that musicians be brought in, and
Magdelon sends for some neighbors so that they may
have a dance. Lucile and Celimene, two neighbor girls,
arrive, along with the musicians. As the dance gets under
way, Du Croisy and La Grange return and begin to beat
their valets. They next remove the fancy clothes worn
by the two masqueraders, leaving them virtually un-
dressed but free to continue their courting of the young
women.

As Mascarille and Jodelet argue with the musicians
over who is to pay them, Gorgibus arrives. Learning of
the trick that has been played on the two young ladies, he
tells them that they deserve such treatment because of
the shameful way in which they have treated their suitors.
Magdelon swears revenge, and as the masqueraders leave,
Mascarille comments that it seems that the young ladies

have no regard for true, unadorned worth, and that they love only outward show.

When the musicians ask Gorgibus for their pay, he gives them a sound beating. Turning then on the girls, he drives them from his sight, saying that their foolish and pretentious ideas have made them all the laughingstock of the town. Alone Gorgibus lashes out at current novels, verses, songs and sonnets as the causes of the girls' folly.

Moliere in the Role of Sganarelle.

SGANARELLE, OR THE IMAGINARY CUCKOLD

SGANARELLE, OR THE IMAGINARY CUCKOLD

(SGANARELLE, OU LE COCU IMAGINAIRE)

CHARACTERS IN THE PLAY

GORGIBUS: father of Celie.

CELIE: in love with Lelie.

CELIE'S MAID

LELIE: in love with Celie.

GROS-RENE: Lelie's valet.

SGANARELLE

SGANARELLE'S WIFE

VILLEBREQUIN: father of Valere.

A RELATIVE OF SGANARELLE'S WIFE

The Scene is in Paris.

As this one-act play begins, Gorgibus is insisting that Celie give up Lelie, to whom she is engaged, and marry Valere, a wealthy and unattractive suitor. Suggesting that Valere's wealth will make him less ugly, Gorgibus tries to convince Celie that with marriage will come the love which she does not now feel toward Valere.

Describing the joys of married life, Celie's maid urges her mistress to accept without hesitation this new suitor. After all, Lelie has been away for some time, and there is no way of knowing when he may return, or whether he may have had a change of heart during his long absence. This is too much for Celie, who suffers a fainting spell. Sganarelle, who happens to be passing by, rushes over and holds Celie in his arms while the maid goes for additional help. From her window Sganarelle's wife sees this woman in her husband's arms, and she hurries to surprise him in the act. Meanwhile, Sganarelle and another man have taken Celie into a nearby house. As she ponders her husband's unfaithfulness, Sganarelle's wife notices something on the ground. It is a portrait which Celie had dropped when she fainted. She picks up the portrait and is examining it when Sganarelle returns to the scene. Unaware of her husband's presence, she places her face close to the portrait to savour the odor. Sganarelle, thinking that she is kissing the portrait, rushes over, snatches it from her hands and accuses her of having a lover. She in turn accuses him of having a mistress. Suddenly she seizes the portrait and runs away, with Sganarelle in close pursuit.

Meanwhile, Lelie arrives with his valet, Gros-Rene. They are both tired and hungry, But Lelie, the typical lover, cannot think of eating at this time. As Gros-Rene leaves to satisfy his hunger, Sganarelle returns with the portrait, which Lelie immediately recognizes as the one he had given to Celie when he left Paris. At the same time Sganarelle recognizes Lelie as the subject of the portrait,

and he rushes away in search of some member of his
wife's family in order to expose her infidelity.

Sganarelle's wife returns, finds Lelie on the verge of
fainting, and assists him in reaching a room in her house
where he can sit down. Sganarelle returns, accompanied
by one of his wife's relatives. The latter, finding no sign
of an alleged lover, refuses to believe Sganarelle's suspicions, but he agrees that the family will certainly punish her if she is guilty. Alone, Sganarelle is trying to convince himself that he is wrong about his wife when suddenly he sees her and Lelie come out of their house. After
stopping to talk briefly, the two separate, and Lelie,
greeting Sganarelle with the rather ambiguous remark,
"how nice to have such a beautiful 'femme' ", proceeds
down the street.

Celie comes out in time to see Lelie speak to Sganarelle. She approaches and asks Sganarelle how it is that
he knows this man. Sganarelle replies that it is not he,
but his wife, who knows Lelie, and that the two adore each
other. Celie then describes her great affliction in such a
manner that Sganarelle thinks she is describing his own
suffering. Finally she leaves, swearing vengeance, which
Sganarelle mistakenly interprets to be in his behalf.
Stirred by this apparent demonstration of sympathy, he
decides to take matters into his own hands. Before doing
anything drastic, however, he pauses to consider the con-
sequences. Reaching the conclusion that he will be the one
who will suffer most in the long run, he seems on the
verge of dropping the whole idea, when suddenly he
changes his mind and decides to go through with his plan,
the first step in which will be to spread the rumor that
Lelie is sleeping with Sganarelle's wife.

Celie, convinced that Lelie has deserted her for Sganarelle's wife, agrees to honor her father's request and
marry Valere. As she is about to explain to her aston-

A Scene from Sganarelle

ished maid the sudden change of heart, Lelie arrives. The scene, one of mutual recrimination, is interrupted by the arrival of Sganarelle. Armed from head to foot and vowing to kill his rival, Sganarelle shows that he is a complete coward when he comes face to face with Lelie. The latter denies that he has any interest whatsoever in Sganarelle's wife, who arrives at this point and begins to accuse Celie of being her husband's mistress. Celie's maid places herself between Lelie and Celie in an attempt to straighten things out. Just as everything seems to be cleared up, Celie suddenly remembers that she has promised to marry Valere.

Gorgibus arrives, refuses to honor the promise made to Lelie, and again demands that Celie marry Valere. At this moment Villebrequin, father of Valere, arrives with the news that his son has been married now for four months and that the agreement is off, whereupon Gorgibus counters with the statement that for some time his daughter has been promised to Lelie and that no other will be acceptable to him as a son-in-law.

Sganarelle's final advice to the young couple is that they learn a lesson from this experience, and that they never believe anything they see, for things are not always what they seem.

DON GARCIA OF NAVARRE

DON GARCIA OF NAVARRE

(DOM GARCIE DE NAVARRE)

CHARACTERS IN THE PLAY

DON GARCIE: Prince of Navarre, in love with Elvire.

ELVIRE: Prince of Leon.

ELISE: confidante of Elvire.

DON ALPHONSE: Prince of Leon; known also as Don Sylve, Prince of Castile.

IGNES: countess, in love with Don Sylve; beloved by Mauregat, the usurper of the throne of Leon.

DON ALVAR: confidant of Don Garcie; in love with Elise.

DON LOPE: another confidant of Don Garcie; rejected lover of Elise.

DON PEDRE: gentleman-usher to Ignes.

The Scene is in Astorga, a City of Spain, in the Kingdom of Leon.

ACT I.

Elvire, Princess of Leon, tries to choose between Don Garcie of Navarre, a worthy but extremely jealous suitor, and Don Sylve, thought to be the Prince of Castile, but who is in reality Don Alphonse, Prince of Leon. Elvire has been aided by Garcie since the death of her father and the loss of the throne of Leon, and she believes that should her brother, now absent in Castile, return to claim the throne, Garcie would be on his side in the struggle against the present usurpers.

Garcie arrives and in a dialogue with Elvire demonstrates a deep jealousy of Sylve. According to rumors, the latter is on his way in command of an army to oust the enemies of Elvire. In order to cure Garcie of his insane and unwarranted jealousy, Elvire finally has to confess her love for him, a thing which a woman of her state should not be required to do.

A letter delivered to Elvire at this moment causes Garcie to react in such a jealous manner that Elvire insists that he read the letter himself to see that he has no cause for jealousy. The letter is, in fact, from Ignes, who is in love with Sylve, and who is being courted by Mauregat, the usurper. Despite urgings from all around her, Ignes would prefer to die rather than consent to marry Mauregat.

Elvire warns Garcie that she is tired of his jealousy, and that she might not be as willing next time to go so far as she has this time in order to prove him wrong. Garcie promises to believe in her from now on and to stop being jealous.

ACT II.

Elise cannot understand why Lope, confidant of Garcie, creates and nurtures suspicions in the mind of the prince, knowing that jealousy is a vice odious to the one being courted by Garcie. Lope explains that the way for a courtier to get along with his master is to flatter him and to tell him what he wants to hear. Since Garcie lives and thrives on suspicions, Lope sees that he is fed a constant diet of disquieting notices and situations.

Garcie arrives for another confrontation with Elvire. He has found the left half of a sheet of paper on which are the halves of a number of lines of verse written in Elvire's hand. Garcie insists on knowing to whom the verses were directed. Elvire decides to teach him a lesson. Elise has the other half of the letter, which was torn in two by her rejected suitor Lope in a tussle with one of the maids. When Garcie realizes that the lines are from a letter addressed to him, he is duly repentant, but Elvire explains that she has permitted him to read the letter in order to have the opportunity to unsay what there is in the letter in his favor. Garcie apologizes, pleads for understanding and forgiveness, and declares that it is the intensity of his love that leads him to mix fears with hope. He explains further that, "since the less deserving a person is of a desired benefit the more difficult it is to believe that fortune will favor him, one is inclined to doubt one's good fortune." Elvire rejects this explanation, but there is no doubt that it has won for Garcie another pardon and a stay.

At this moment Lope arrives with the news that the people of Leon have heard that the Prince of Castile is coming to their aid, and that they are ready to rise against the tyrant now ruling illegally in their kingdom. Garcie must now plan his campaign in such a way as to get some of the credit. Meanwhile he insists on hearing from Lope a secret concerning his other campaign, that for the hand of Elvire.

ACT III.

Elvire cannot understand why she is so easily led by
Garcie to forgive him time after time. Elise attributes
this weakness to an excess of love on the part of both parties. It is easy to see that Elvire's resentment arises primarily from the fact that she must be constantly confessing her love for Garcie.

Sylve arrives unexpectedly and expresses his regret
to Elvire that a rival for her hand has had the advantage
of being of close personal help to her. Elvire explains that
Castile has done enough in protecting her brother for
twenty years while he was awaiting the opportunity to regain his rightful throne. She tries unsuccessfully to persuade Sylve that he should return Ignes' great love for
him and take her for his wife.

Garcie unexpectedly comes upon the two engaged in
conversation. He chides Sylve for not letting them know of
his coming so that they could have accorded him appropriate honors. The implication is that Sylve wanted his
meeting with Elvire to be a secret, and again jealousy
rears its ugly head. Garcie accuses Elvire of having expected this visit. Elvire counters by making it clear to the
jealous prince that he has no claim on her, and that she
welcomes Sylve's help in punishing the tyrants now in power in Leon.

Garcie, alone with Sylve, declares that if he cannot
have Elvire, he will do all that he can to prevent anyone
else, including Sylve himself, from having her. Sylve
leaves the scene as he had entered, secretly, confident
that fortune will be on his side.

ACT IV.

Alvar, confidant of Garcie, begs Elvire to forgive Garcie this most recent display of jealousy, which he says is

caused by a false report from Lope. Elvire, not convinced, declares that Garcie's alleged suffering is well
deserved.

Ignes, dressed as a man, comes to see Elvire. In order to escape a marriage with Mauregat, she has let the
word be spread that she has killed herself. As Ignes enters a room where Elvire is waiting to receive her, Alvar
brings in Garcie. He hopes to use Elise to help the frustrated prince. Elise refuses to intervene and goes for Elvire so that the latter can herself dismiss the persistent
lover. Through the half-closed door Garcie sees the figure
of a man in the arms of Elvire, and again he is certain
that his beloved is deceiving him. Elvire comes out, expecting to hear excuses and pleadings for forgiveness. Instead she is greeted with rantings and accusations. Realizing that Garcie has seen Ignes in her embrace, Elvire
offers him the alternative of believing her innocent or of
learning who her supposed lover is. If he insists on the
latter alternative the penalty will be permanent banish-
ment from her sight and her love. Garcie is sure that this
is a trick, and his jealousy is so intense that he must see
with his own eyes the cause of his suspicions.

Elvire has Elise bring Ignes out, apologizing to the
latter for having to reveal her secret in order to demon-
strate the falsity of Garcie's suspicions. Swearing never
to see him again, Elvire leaves Garcie remorseful and determined to atone for the offense he has just committed
against his love. He will sacrifice his own life, if need
be, in a spectacular individual attempt on the life of Mauregat. In this way he will at least have the pleasure of de-
priving his supposed rival, Sylve, of the glory of displac-
ing the usurper of the throne of Leon.

ACT V.

Alvar brings the news that Garcie has been foiled in

his plans and that Sylve has reached Mauregat first. In payment for this service, Alphonse plans to give his sister, Elvire, in marriage to Sylve. Elvire has also received a communication which seems to confirm this. Compassion for the unfortunate Garcie causes her to lose her resentment against him, revealing a still smouldering love for the unhappy prince.

Elvire explains to Garcie that she is sorry, in a way, that her brother is regaining the throne, since it means that she must obey him as her king and marry Sylve. Garcie accepts what he and Elvire call this decree of Fate, and he prepares to open the gates of the city to that fortunate conqueror.

Elvire explains to Ignes her regret that the secret love between the latter and Sylve had not been revealed sooner, so that the present undesirable situation could have been avoided.

When Sylve arrives, apparently for the purpose of claiming his prize, Elvire begs him not to accept the new king's offer, and she agrees to enter a convent rather than marry anyone else. Sylve then reveals the well kept secret that he is really Alphonse, and that it was the people themselves who rose up against the usurper when a rumor spread that Sylve and his men had seized the city. Alphonse's concern now is for Ignes, whose whereabouts are unknown to him. Ignes, still dressed as a man, hears Alphonse tell of his love for her and of his desire to make her his queen, whereupon she reveals her identity and agrees to accept him.

Garcie arrives, notes the contentment which Elvire shows in her face, and mistakes this for joy at being in the presence of his rival. Ignes clears up the matter by revealing the identity of Alphonse, who then offers to help Garcie. The latter expects nothing good to come of his efforts, and he is pleasantly surprise when Elvire makes clear her willingness to forgive and forget; whereupon the new king promises a marriage which will join not only their hearts but also their respective kingdoms.

THE SCHOOL FOR HUSBANDS

THE SCHOOL FOR HUSBANDS

(L'ECOLE DES MARIS)

CHARACTERS IN THE PLAY

SGANARELLE: younger brother of Ariste and guardian of Isabelle.

ARISTE: guardian of Leonor.

ISABELLE: sister of Leonor and ward of Sganarelle.

LEONOR: ward of Ariste.

LISETTE: Leonor's maid.

VALERE: in love with Isabelle.

ERGASTE: Valere's valet.

MAGISTRATE

NOTARY

TWO FOOTMEN

The Scene is a Public Square in Paris.

ACT I.

In fulfillment of the deathbed wish of their father, Isabelle and Leonor are being brought up by Sganarelle and Ariste, who are expected either to marry their respective wards or to find husbands for them.

Since each of the brothers hopes to marry his ward, he is careful to bring her up in the way he judges best to prepare her for marriage. The play opens with Sganarelle and Ariste discussing the difference in the way each is bringing up his ward. Sganarelle has been extremely harsh and strict in his methods, while Ariste has been very lenient and tolerant. Ariste is trying to convince Sganarelle that he is too severe, even in his manner of dress, and that he should get in step with the times and conform to the customs of society.

Leonor, Isabelle and Lisette arrive on the scene, unnoticed at first by Sganarelle and Ariste. They are discussing the fact that Isabelle is normally kept locked in her room when not in the company of her guardian. Upon being discovered by Sganarelle, Leonor explains that the three girls are planning to go out for some fresh air. Despite Ariste's pleading, Sganarelle refuses to permit Isabelle to go out with Leonor and Lisette; he proceeds to condemn Ariste's methods and to defend his own in preparing his young ward to be a proper wife. He even suggests that Leonor is spoiling Isabelle and asks that she not visit her again.

Lisette accuses Sganarelle of not trusting Isabelle and of treating her in the manner of Turkish women. Ariste defends the girls and their ideas and tells Sganarelle that honor, not chains, keeps women virtuous, and that one must win the heart of a woman in order to gain her trust. Society is a better teacher than books, according to Ariste, and he is permitting Leonor to learn and to decide for

herself. If she decides to choose a younger man for a husband, Ariste will not oppose her will. If she casts her lot
with him, he will not be more strict with her after marriage than before. All this brings Sganarelle to predict
that Ariste will assuredly be deceived by such a wife;
however, Leonor assures Ariste that if she chooses him,
she will always be faithful. All leave except Sganarelle,
who expresses his contempt for such thinking and indicates that he has not changed his mind at all.

Valere and his valet Ergaste arrive, unnoticed at first
by Sganarelle, who continues to ponder over the corrupt-
ness of the present-day society. Finally Valere gains his
attention, explains that he is a new neighbor, and begins
to ask him about his habits. He promises to pay Sganarelle
a visit soon, and the latter leaves. Valere is enraged to
think that his beloved, Isabelle, is in the power of such a
savage. Ergaste explains that this gives Valere an advantage over Sganarelle in his quest. Valere has followed her
for four months without being able to speak to her even
once. With his eyes he has tried to tell her of his great
love for her, but in the absence of servants to bribe, he
has been unable to determine whether she has understood.
Ergaste suggests that they go home and work out a plan.

ACT II.

Isabelle has noticed Valere, and she plans to find a
way to meet him. When she mentions the new neighbor to
her guardian, Sganarelle decides to have a showdown with
this young man and goes to see him at his house. Refusing
either to enter the house or to accept a chair offered him,
Sganarelle insists that Valere listen to him. The elder
man explains to Valere that he must not become attentive
to Isabelle since she is destined to become Sganarelle's
wife.

Sganarelle innocently relates to Valere Isabelle's message that she has noticed and understood the looks given her by Valere and wishes him to desist in his efforts to communicate with her. What Sganarelle does not know is that in Isabelle's message there is a hidden meaning which Valere and Ergaste recognize. As Valere and his valet excuse themselves, Sganarelle, unaware of the part he has played in Isabelle's scheme, congratulates himself on the results of his method.

On his return home Sganarelle reports to Isabelle on the results of his mission, assuring her that her admirer will not bother her again. Isabelle says that she fears the opposite, since hardly was Sganarelle out of the house when a messenger tossed through her open window a box containing a letter from Valere. She wishes the letter returned unopened to its writer as soon as possible in order to show her disdain for him. When Sganarelle tells her that she has learned her lesson well and is worthy of being his wife, Isabelle then tells Sganarelle that he may open the letter if he wishes. The latter, deceived by the apparent goodwill of his ward, delivers the letter post haste to Ergaste without opening it. In the letter Isabelle tells Valere that she is threatened with an undesired marriage to her guardian within six days and in desperation is appealing to him for help in avoiding such a catastrophe.

Unaware of what the letter contains, Sganarelle chides Valere for having thought that he could succeed in his scheme. Valere then proceeds to flatter Sganarelle to such an extent that the latter agrees to take back to Isabelle the message that Valere's intentions have been honorable, and that his only hope was to make her his wife, that he will always remember and love her, and that only a formidable obstacle in the person of such a redoubtable rival as Sganarelle could have caused him to give up the fight for

her. The apparent sincerity of Valere's words actually
moves Sganarelle to pity his poor rival.

Sganarelle gives Isabelle the message, exactly as dic-
tated by Valere. Isabelle chides Sganarelle for pitying
Valere, recounting now a rumor she has just heard to the
effect that the young man is planning to prevent her coming marriage by entering her room and carrying her off.
Sganarelle, pleased with the apparent discretion of his
ward, promises to go immediately to speak to Valere of
this latest threat to his happiness.

After accusing Valere of planning to carry Isabelle
off, Sganarelle tells him that Isabelle again insists that he
stop trying to see her. Valere says that if what Sganarelle
says is true, then he will desist. To prove to Valere that
he is telling the truth, Sganarelle takes his rival to hear
from her own lips the decision of Isabelle.

In a cleverly contrived scene, typical of Moliere, Isabelle and Valere make clear their love for each other
through words that can be understood in two ways as Sganarelle, completely unaware that he is being duped, hears
Valere say that within three days Isabelle will be rid of
something that is odious to her. Sganarelle, again feeling
pity for his defeated rival, embraces Valere. Alone with
Isabelle and carried away by what he thinks is her fond
regard for him, Sganarelle declares that they will not wait
any longer, but that they will be married the next day.

ACT III.

It is now night and Isabelle, preferring death to a life
of marriage with Sganarelle, decides to commit her fate
to her lover and prepares to go to him. She is intercepted
by Sganarelle, whereupon she quickly makes up a story
concerning Leonor and Valere. The two have been in love
for a year, according to Isabelle, and Leonor is even now

locked in Isabelle's room preparing to meet Valere tonight in the alley just outside her window in order to try to win him back from Isabelle. Pretending that she had tried to dissuade Leonor, Isabelle says that she has finally given in to the scheme and that she is now on her way to get a friend, Lucrece, to come and stay with her tonight. Sganarelle, fearing for his honor should Isabelle be seen, refuses to let her go outside. Isabelle then offers to make Leonor leave the house, but she insists that Sganarelle hide and that he not speak to Leonor as he watches her leave. Sganarelle agrees, Isabelle enters her room, pretends to upbraid her sister and orders her out. Isabelle, disguised as Leonor and protected by darkness, then leaves the house. Sganarelle follows her to Valere's house where he overhears her tell Valere that she is Isabelle; however, he thinks that she is only trying to trick Valere.

In order to save his own and his brother's honor, Sganarelle goes for a magistrate to have the couple married. While the magistrate and the notary wait outside Valere's house, Sganarelle goes for his brother Ariste so that the latter can witness the ceremony. Ariste cannot believe what he hears and insists that Leonor is attending a dance. He does, however, accompany Sganarelle to Valere's house. Sganarelle convinces Ariste that the two young people must marry at once in order to preserve the honor of the family. Ariste, placing the wishes of his ward above his own desires, agrees.

Valere has hidden Isabelle in a separate room and insists that all papers be signed agreeing to the marriage before permitting the others to enter the house. Ariste attempts to find out whether the person is really Leonor, but Sganarelle prevents him from getting an answer. Finally all parties concerned, including Ariste, sign the marriage contract on which the name of the bride is left blank. At this moment Leonor enters the room. She has returned early from the ball because she was bored with the young blades. Both Sganarelle and Ariste assume that she is the girl kept hidden by Valere. Ariste chides her for not having confided in him her love for Valere. Leonor does not understand. She assures Ariste that she loves only him and wishes to marry him as soon as possible.

Isabelle comes out, reveals that she has tricked Sganarelle, and asks her sister's forgiveness for having involved her in the scheme. All are pleased at the way things have turned out, all, that is, except Sganarelle. For him all women are devils and are not to be trusted. Ariste invites everyone to his house to celebrate the occasion, and Lisette, speaking to the audience, invites distressed husbands to come to school at their place.

THE BORES

THE BORES

(LES FACHEUX)

CHARACTERS IN THE PLAY

ERASTE: in love with Orphise.

ORPHISE

LA MONTAGNE: valet of Eraste.

DAMIS: guardian of Orphise.

L'ESPINE: valet of Damis.

THE BORES: Alcidor, Lysandre, Alcandre, Alcippe, Orante, Clymene, Dorante, Caritides, Ormin, Filinte.

LA RIVIERE AND TWO OTHER SERVANTS OF ERASTE

The Scene is in Paris.

Having little or no plot and a series of virtually uncon-
nected scenes, this play has as its purpose the presentation of a procession of "bores" commonly found in the
court of France in 1661. The single thread which hold the
story together is the desire of Eraste to be with Orphise,
a desire which is repeatedly frustrated and finally ful-
filled.

ACT I.

The first act opens with Eraste telling La Montagne
about an annoying experience which he has just had with
a young nobleman, an insufferable bore, during the course
of a theatrical performance. And speaking of bores, he
considers Damis, uncle and guardian of Orphise, as the
worst of all, principally because Damis thwarts all his
efforts to court that young lady. Now even La Montagne's
fastidiousness in preparing his master for an appointment
annoys Eraste and tries his patience.

Orphise, on the arm of Alcidor, a gentleman of the
court, passes Eraste on the street without so much as a
look in his direction. Eraste, in disbelief, sends La Montagne to follow them and report back his findings. Meanwhile Lysander gets Eraste's ear and annoys him with his
singing and dancing and with his comments on a "courante"
which he has recently composed. Eraste gets rid of him
as La Montagne returns, followed by Orphise. The latter
explains that she only accepted Alcidor's assist to her
carriage in order to rid herself of him, and that she returned immediately by another gate in order to be with
Eraste.

At this point Alcandre, another bore, interrupts, caus-
ing Orphise to leave. Alcandre wants Eraste to carry a
challenge from him to a man who has just insulted him.
Eraste refuses, since it is the king's desire to eliminate

duelling among his courtiers. La Montagne goes in search
of Orphise, and Eraste waits as the curtain falls.

ACT II.

As the second act begins, Alcippe arrives and bores
Eraste with a lengthy tale of how he lost an incredible
game at cards. Ridding himself at last of this troublesome
pest, Eraste listens impatiently as La Montagne finally
gets around to telling him that Orphise will see him there
as soon as she can get rid of some country ladies who are
bothering her. As Eraste awaits the arrival of his beloved,
Orante and Clymene approach and ask him to settle an
argument they have been having as to which is the greater
lover, one who is jealous, or one who is not. Eraste listens to their endless debate until he feels that he must
give an opinion in order to get rid of them. His answer,
that the jealous loves most and the other loves best, does
not really satisfy either. Meanwhile, Orphise arrives,
sees Eraste engaged in conversation, and excuses herself, saying that she does not wish to interrupt.

As Eraste ponders the incomprehensible weaker sex,
Dorante arrives to tell a long and detailed story of a hunt,
which finally ends when a country clod shoots the stag
with a pistol.

ACT III.

As the third and final act opens, Eraste is looking for-
ward to his secret appointment this evening with Orphise.
Caritides, a pedantic scholar who scorns those whose
names have the Latin ending "US", and who prides himself on having a name with a Greek ending, comes to ask
a favor of Eraste. He wants the latter to carry a petition
to the king, criticizing the spelling of inscriptions through-

Scene from The Bores.

out the country, and requesting appointment of Caritides
to an office with authority to correct all these errors.

Eraste succeeds in getting rid of Caritides, only to
find himself the victim of another bore, Ormin, who promises to make him a fortune. Since the king receives such
a vast sum annually from the country's seaports, Ormin's
plan is to turn all the coasts of France into famous seaports. For revealing this secret to Eraste, Ormin asks
only a couple of pieces of silver, and Eraste wishes he
could get rid of all such nuisances as cheaply.

Filinte has heard that Eraste has been challenged to a
duel, and he refuses to leave his side for a minute. Unable to convince Filinte that this evening's affair is not one
of honor, but of the heart, Eraste finally hits upon a means
of ridding himself of this undesirable companion by declaring that Filinte is the one with whom he has the quarrel.

Eraste arrives for his appointment, only to find that
Damis has learned of the secret meeting and is waiting at
the door to Orphise's room. La Riviere and the other servants attack Damis when they overhear him giving instructions to his men to kill Eraste. However, Eraste's honor
requires that he help the guardian of his beloved. When
Damis realizes that it is Eraste who has saved his life,
he has a change of heart and agrees to give Orphise to
Eraste in marriage.

THE SCHOOL FOR WIVES

THE SCHOOL FOR WIVES

(L'ECOLE DES FEMMES)

CHARACTERS IN THE PLAY

ARNOLPHE: age 42, also known as M. de la Souche.

AGNES: 17, ward of Arnolphe.

HORACE: young man, in love with Agnes.

ALAIN: servant of Arnolphe.

GEORGETTE: servant girl of Arnolphe.

CHRYSALDE: friend of Arnolphe.

ENRIQUE: brother-in-law of Chrysalde.

ORONTE: father of Horace and old friend of Arnolphe.

A NOTARY

The Scene is a Town Square in France.

ACT I.

The play opens with Arnolphe telling his old friend Chrysalde of his plans to be married soon. Chrysalde tries to dissuade Arnolphe, reminding him that he runs the risk not only of being deceived by his wife, but also that of being laughed at by the husbands whom he has long criticized for being so tolerant with their wayward wives. Arnolphe explains that he has taken care of this. Agnes, the bride to be, has been brought up by Arnolphe since she was four years old, first in a convent and later in his own household. On the theory that a clever wife is a dangerous wife, he has seen to it that she is innocent, unspoiled, and ignorant of the ways of the world, particularly of men.

On a whim, Arnolphe has recently changed his name. He now wishes to be called M. de la Souche. Few people know of this change. Most of his friends and acquaintances, including Agnes, know him as Arnolphe. When Arnolphe reaches his house, he has to threaten his two lazy servants, Alain and Georgette, before they will let him in. He has been absent for ten days, and when he asks about Agnes, he receives a vague reply. Agnes comes down, holding some needlework in her hands, and Arnolphe is reassured. Sending her back upstairs, he tells her that he will return soon to discuss with her some important matters. Alone, he contrasts this paragon of virtue with learned women who know how to speak and write elegantly.

At this moment Horace, the son of Oronte, an old friend of Arnolphe, enters the room. Arnolphe is shocked to learn that Horace has been living in his house for nine days. On inquiring about his old friend, Arnolphe learns that Enrique, a fellow townsman, absent in America for the past fourteen years, is arriving soon with Oronte on a matter of some importance. Horace takes advantage

of Arnolphe's present g e n e r o u s mood to borrow some
money. When Arnolphe asks Horace whether he has not
had some amorous adventures since arriving, the latter
replies that he has indeed been well received by a charming young lady who lives in a small house next to Arnolphe's, and who is kept hidden from the world by some ridiculous old man named de la Souche. Horace explains
to a stupefied Arnolphe that he plans to use the money
just received to further his plans with this girl, whose
name is Agnes, and he swears Arnolphe to secrecy about
the matter. Alone, Arnolphe realizes that he has not
asked enough questions to find out just how far this affair
has gone, and he decides to try to overtake Horace, even
though, as he says, we often seek more than we wish to
find.

ACT II.

Arnolphe fails to catch up with Horace and returns
home. Having determined to marry Agnes, he already
considers any slip on her part a blot on his own honor.
On entering his house, he curses and threatens his two
servants and accuses them of treachery. When Arnolphe
leaves to ask Agnes to come for a walk with him, Alain
tries to explain to Georgette why Arnolphe is so furious
with them. It is jealousy.

Arnolphe and Agnes go for a walk. After some small
talk, Arnolphe asks about the young man who has been
staying in the house for the past several days. Agnes tells
a completely innocent story of how she came to invite
this young man in after an old woman had told her that
she was the only person who could cure a disease caused
by the sight of her eyes. Agnes says that the young man
has been cured of his disease each time that he has visited her. Unable to talk with her in terms which he would

like to use, Arnolphe asks whether the young man has taken anything from her. After several exchanges, at the end of which Arnolphe is suffering the torments of the damned, Agnes finally admits that the young man has taken a ribbon. Somewhat relieved, Arnolphe then asks whether the young man has asked for any other remedy for his disorder. In her innocence Agnes says that she would have granted him anything to help him, if he had asked for it.

Arnolphe realizes that he has made a mistake and that he is lucky to have come out as well as he has in this instance. He explains to Agnes that accepting gifts, listening to the deceitful words of handsome young men, and accepting their caresses are mortal sins taken away only by marriage. Agnes then wishes to be married. When Arnolphe says that he will marry her this very evening, she misunderstands and thinks that he means to marry her to the handsome young man. Shocked, Arnolphe explains that he has another in mind as her husband. He forbids her to see this young man again, and instructs her to close the door in his face and throw a stone out of the window at him if he knocks.

ACT III.

Arnolphe is pleased to have seen Agnes throw a stone at Horace, and he determines not to delay the marriage further. Sending the servants away in search of a notary, he discusses with Agnes the role of a wife in marriage. After explaining in some detail how the wife must always be subservient to the husband, he gives her a book to read on the duties of a wife. She reads aloud the first ten maxims, after which Arnolphe dismisses her to continue her reading. Alone, he congratulates himself on his choice of a wife. Agnes is like wax in his hands, and he will be able to give her whatever shape he wishes.

Horace arrives with the news that things have not
been going well in his affair with Agnes. Her governor
has returned from the country and has discovered the
affair. Her door is barred to him, and she has even thrown
a stone at him. However, it seems that love has done marvels for this simple girl, for she had attached a letter to
the stone. Arnolphe is not amused as Horace praises the
girl and ridicules her would-be protector. Finally he permits Arnolphe to read the letter, which is a model of innocence, and in which Agnes expresses her desire to be
always near Horace and her refusal to believe those who
are trying to warn her that he is planning to deceive her.

Arnolphe is disturbed by what he has just learned.
Horace, after threatening to deal harshly with the scoun-
drel who is stifling the spirit of such a lovely creature,
asks Arnolphe to aid him in getting into the house where
Agnes lives. Arnolphe cannot help him, but he is confident
that Horace will find someone who can. Alone, Arnolphe
feels defeated and betrayed. He considers freeing Agnes,
leaving her to a certain evil fate, and thereby gaining
revenge on her for her treachery. But he cannot give up
so easily something he loves. In spite of the base trick
which she has played on him, he loves her too much to
hurt her.

ACT IV.

Arnolphe has just come from a visit to Agnes' room,
where he found himself unable to utter a word, despite
the fury that he felt upon observing her, cool, calm, and
unrepentant. She was also lovelier than ever, and Arnolphe, his passion rekindled, has decided to fight for his
interests.

As Arnolphe paces the floor talking aloud to himself,
a notary, called earlier for the purpose of drawing up the

marriage contract, arrives with his portfolio. In a scene of the type in which Moliere excels. Arnolphe continues to ponder over his problem, completely unaware of the presence of the notary, as the latter, thinking that each comment or question of Arnolphe refers to the marriage agreement, replies in such a way that he describes just how a marriage contract should be drawn up.

Suddenly Arnolphe notices the presence of the notary and, realizing what is happening, abruptly he decides to postpone the matter. He dismisses the notary and leaves the room. He returns shortly thereafter, and in another typically Molieresque scene, the servants, replying to Arnolphe's questions as to how they would respond to H o r a c e, should the latter try to bribe them with fine speeches and gifts, reveal what they really think of their master.

The servants leave the scene, and Arnolphe plans his campaign. Horace interrupts to tell Arnolphe that he was secretly hidden in Agnes' room at the time her jealous suitor entered in a rage. Since no words were spoken, Horace does not realize that the visitor was Arnolphe, and he innocently tells how he is to enter her room again that very night without making a noise. Alone, Arnolphe wonders how, after twenty years of study in how to avoid the troubles other men have experienced, he could be defeated by a simple girl and a scatterbrained young fellow. He plans to take advantage of this blunder which his rival has just made in revealing his plans.

Chrysalde, finding his friend Arnolphe a bit upset and touchy, chides him for his obsession about men who permit their wives to deceive them. He suggests that Arnolphe be willing to accept a mean position in the matter. He even suggests that cuckoldom is sometimes better than life with a holier-than-thou woman. Arnolphe again refuses to accept such a philosophy, and he arranges with

his two servants to lay a trap for Horace tonight and beat
him as he tries to enter Agnes' room by means of a ladder. Alone, he remarks that if all the husbands in the
town received their wives' lovers in this way, there would
be fewer cases of deceived husbands.

ACT V.

As Horace reaches the top of the ladder, the servants
attempt to strike him. The poor fellow loses his footing
and falls to the ground. When everyone rushes below to
see what has happened, Horace pretends to be dead. Back
in the house Arnolphe now upbraids his servants for being
so rough in handling the situation. As the servants leave,
Horace arrives to explain how he has fooled his rival,
along with his servants, and that Agnes, upon hearing the
commotion, has come to his aid. He asks Arnolphe to take
her into his house to protect her.

Arnolphe, his face concealed and his voice disguised,
drags Agnes away from Horace and into the house. There
he reveals himself and reprimands her for her ungrateful conduct. In a delightful scene Agnes counters all of
Arnolphe's attacks with the most naive and honest answers, explaining that Horace has made himself attract-
ive by painting a beautiful picture of love and marriage,
whereas Arnolphe has presented a dismal picture of what
life would be with him. Arnolphe threatens to send her
away. Alain arrives and Arnolphe orders him to guard
Agnes in his room until he can arrange to have her taken
to a safe place.

Horace returns with the news that Oronte has arranged
for him to marry the daughter of Enrique, and he asks
Arnolphe's aid in thwarting his father's plans. Arnolphe
agrees to help Horace, but when Oronte, Enrique, and
Chrysalde arrive to discuss the matter, Arnolphe urges

A Scene from The School for Wives.

Oronte to impose his parental authority on Horace and insist on the marriage. When Arnolphe is revealed to be also M. de la Souche, Horace realizes that he is in trouble. Agnes tries to escape, but she is apprehended and is brought to say good-bye to Horace before being carried away. Oronte now reveals that the daughter of Enrique is a member of Arnolphe's household. She had been left with a country woman thirteen years before when she was four years old and has recently been traced to Arnolphe. Agnes is, of course, this daughter, and her love for Horace will have a happy ending. Arnolphe leaves the scene in a rage as Chrysalde tells him that the only way to avoid becoming a cuckold is not to marry. As the curtain falls, Chrysalde gives thanks to Heaven, which orders all for the best.

THE FORCED MARRIAGE

THE FORCED MARRIAGE

(LE MARIAGE FORCE)

CHARACTERS IN THE PLAY

SGANARELLE

GERONIMO: friend of Sganarelle.

DORIMENE: young coquette betrothed to Sganarelle.

ALCANTOR: father of Dorimene.

ALCIDAS: brother of Dorimene.

LYCASTE: in love with Dorimene.

PANCRACE: an Aristotelian Doctor.

MARPHURIUS: a Pyrrhonian Doctor.

TWO GYPSY WOMEN

Sganarelle is thinking of getting married, and he asks his friend Geronimo for his opinion on the matter. When Geronimo asks Sganarelle how old he is, the latter pretends not to know. Some detailed calculations, however, produce a figure of fifty-two. Geronimo feels that a man who has managed to avoid the chains of marriage for so long should not give up his freedom now. However, when Sganarelle explains that he is determined to marry, that he has chosen the girl, and that her father has given his consent, Geronimo reverses himself and agrees that Sganarelle must marry, by all means. Sganarelle then speaks of the joy which this marriage will bring to him, the children who will carry on his name, and the care which his young wife will give him. Geronimo is overjoyed when he learns that the bride-to-be is Dorimene. He promises to attend the wedding, and he is sure that it will be a happy match.

Sganarelle chances to meet up with Dorimene, who is on her way to do some shopping. He reminds her that soon she will be his, all his. He describes her many charms, and asks whether she is not happy at the prospect of marriage with him. Her reply indicates that her primary interest is to escape the restraints now imposed on her by her father, and she expects that the marital relationship into which she is about to enter will be so free that she will be able to enjoy all the pleasures now denied to her. Such an attitude on the part of his betrothed disturbs Sganarelle, and he pales noticeably. Dorimene assures him that marriage will take care of his illness.

His ardor somewhat diminished, Sganarelle tries to explain his misgivings to Geronimo. The latter suggests that he discuss the matter with the two philosophers Pancrace and Marphurius.

Sganarelle seeks out first Pancrace, whom he finds in the act of haranguing an opponent who has not followed

Aristotle's method and hence has not reasoned properly. The current problem seems to be whether one says the "figure" of a hat or the "form" of a hat. Pancrace insists on the former, since a hat is an inanimate object and the term "form" should be applied only to inanimate beings. Sganarelle, unable at first to get Pancrace's attention to his own problem, finally takes his side against the opponent. The doctor then agrees to listen to his question, but only after determining which language they are to use in discussing the matter. When Sganarelle suggests French as the idiom to be used, Pancrace asks Sganarelle to place himself so that his words will fall upon the ear used for speech in the vulgar tongues rather than upon the ear reserved for classical languages.

He then suggests several philosophical questions which Sganarelle must wish to discuss. Nothing could be farther from Sganarelle's mind, but when he tries to present his problem, Pancrace pays no attention to him and launches into a philosophical discussion of "la parole," which he describes variously as : the portrait of our thoughts, the interpreter of one's heart, the image of the soul, a mirror which reveals our innermost secrets. The doctor implores Sganarelle to make use of that great gift to man to express what he is thinking. Sganarelle, of course, has been trying to do that very thing. He has attempted to interrupt the loquacious doctor by every means possible up to this time. Enraged by Pancrace's insistence that the Aristotelian method be used in presenting his case, Sganarelle picks up some stones and threatens the doctor with bodily harm. Pancrace insists that Sganarelle will never be anything but a numbskull, and he proceeds to extol his own virtues and his abilities in the many fields of philosophy and of knowledge. Sganarelle decides to consult the other scholar.

Marphurius, a Pyrrhonian Doctor, explains that his

philosophy demands that no proposition be stated decisively, that everything should be spoken with uncertainty, and that judgments should always be suspended. For that reason Sganarelle must not say that he has come to seek his advice, but rather that he only thinks he has come for that purpose. Sganarelle cannot understand this kind of reasoning, but he decides to get to the point and present his problem. Marphurius responds to every question or suggestion with an evasive answer or an irrelevant comment. When he finally insists on washing his hands of the whole matter, leaving Sganarelle to do as he pleases, the latter attacks the old philosopher with a stick. When Marphurius complains about the beating, Sganarelle insists that he should only say that he thinks he has received a beating. Giving the doctor a dose of his own medicine, Sganarelle shows that there is no certainty that the latter has been beaten, and he washes his hands of the matter. As Sganarelle ponders what to do next, he spies some Gypsies nearby, and he decides to consult them concerning his future.

Two Gypsy women stop their singing and dancing in order to listen to Sganarelle. They assure him that he will be married soon, to a gentle wife, who will be caressed and loved by everyone, and who will bring him friends and a great reputation. Disturbed at the possible meaning of these announcements, Sganarelle asks whether that means he will become a cuckold. The Gypsy women evade the question, resume their singing and dancing, and leave Sganarelle even more perplexed than before. Just then he sees Lycaste and Dorimene approaching.

Lycaste cannot understand why Dorimene is marrying someone else, considering the great love they share and the promises made between them. Dorimene explains that she is marrying for money, not for love, and that within six months her husband will die, leaving her rich and free to enjoy the happy condition of widowhood. Lycaste, seeing Sganarelle nearby and learning that he is the husband-to-be, hastens over to congratulate him, to wish him the best, and to assure him that he is marrying a worthy lady. As the other two leave, Sganarelle decides that marriage at this time would be a mistake.

Sganarelle now goes to see Alcantor, his future father-in-law, and tries to get out of the marriage. He explains that he is too old for the girl and that she could never be happy with him. Alcantor refuses to break the engagement, whereupon Sganarelle declares that, like his father and his father's father before him, he will never marry. Alcantor enters his house to think the matter over, and Sganarelle, pleasantly surprised at the ease with which he has apparently been able to avoid a bad situation, congratulates himself for having made such a wise decision.

Alcidas, brother of Dorimene, comes out shortly and offers Sganarelle a choice between marriage and duelling. Sganarelle, misled by the calm manner in which the challenge is presented, refuses to fight, whereupon Alcidas gives him a beating. Renewing the offer of a sword which he has brought for the occasion, Alcidas again insists that Sganarelle fight or marry Dorimene. Refusing a second time, Sganarelle receives another beating, after which he agrees to the marriage. Alcidas calls his father, who comes out of the house, accompanied by Dorimene. Plans are made for the wedding, and Alcantor, pleased to be rid of his daughter, will lead the rejoicing at the celebration of this ''happy'' marriage.

THE PRINCESS OF ELIS

THE PRINCESS OF ELIS

(LA PRINCESSE D'ELIDE)

CHARACTERS IN THE PLAY

THE PRINCESS OF ELIS

AGLANTE: cousin of the Princess.

CYNTHIE: cousin of the Princess.

PHILIS: the Princess' maid.

IPHITAS: father of the Princess.

EURYALE: Prince of Ithaca.

ARISTOMENE: Prince of Messene.

THEOCLE: Prince of Pylos.

ARBATE: "gouverneur" to the Prince of Ithica.

MORON: the Princess' favorite buffoon.

LYCAS: servant of Iphitas.

Additional characters appearing in the Prologue and in the Interludes.

AURORA
LYCISCAS: huntsman.
THREE HUNTSMEN
A SATYR
TIRCIS: In some editions: THYRSIS.
CLYMENE

The Scene is in Elis, in Ancient Greece.

In a Prologue, the love song of Aurora awakens three
sleeping huntsmen, who in turn awaken Lyciscas, and they
all begin to prepare for the hunt. This event is part of a
celebration planned by the Prince of Elis, and to which he
has invited the Princes of Ithaca, Messene and Pylos, in
the hope that one of these will please his daughter, the
Princess, and become her husband. The Princess, an ar-
dent lover of the hunt, as well as of all kinds of sporting
events, has shown nothing but disdain and contempt up to
now for all pretenders to her hand.

ACT I.

As the play opens, Euryale is explaining to his "gouverneur," Arbate, how the reputation of the Princess for
haughtiness has caused such wonderment in his mind that
he has developed an inexplicable passion for her. He has
accepted the invitation of her father in order to see whether he can succeed where others have failed in conquering
the disdain of this woman. Fearful of being rejected if he
attempts a direct approach, he has employed the Princess'
favorite buffoon, Moron, to help in his undertaking.
    At this moment the frightened voice of Moron is heard
close by. A boar, pursued by the hunters, has surprised
him in the midst of a nap, and has caused him to drop his
arms and flee the pursuing beast. His explanation of his
actions shows him to be the typical c l o w n, cowardly as
well as humorous. He would prefer that people should say:
"it was here that Moron by flying saved himself from the
fury of a wild boar" rather than "in this illustrious place
the brave Moron, facing a furious boar with heroic bold-
ness, died as the result of a blow from the tusks of the
vicious animal." As for the affair of the Princess, Moron
has not yet found the right moment to speak for Euryale.
As a former Ithacan, however, he reaffirms his loyalty to

the young ruler, and he even hints that he and Euryale may be brothers. Moron recalls that his "mother's husband" used to brag among the shepherds about how the former Prince, father of Euryale, sometimes called at their house during his travels.

Aristomene, Prince of Messene, rescues the Princess from the fury of a wild boar. Instead of showing gratitude, the Princess shows anger at being deprived of the pleasure of killing the beast with her bow and arrow. Euryale witnesses the scene in disbelief. Bidding Moron and Arbate follow him, he promises to reveal to them a plan he has devised for conquering this proud Diana.

In an Interlude between Acts I and II, Moron leaves his Prince in order to speak to the woods and the rocks concerning his passion for Philis, the Princess' maid. As the sound of the name "Philis" echoes back and forth, a bear suddenly appears. In the amusing scene which follows, Moron bows reverently to the bear, flatters him with compliments on his beauty and charm, and then quickly climbs a tree as a group of hunters arrives. The hunters kill the bear, after which Moron climbs down to share in the triumph over the unfortunate beast.

ACT II.

The scene is a peaceful retreat outside the city's walls. Inside, preparations are being made for the chariot race in which the three princes will be competing. The Princess, in the company of her cousins Aglante and Cynthie, praises the beauties of nature and resists the urgings of her cousins, who are trying to persuade her to return for the spectacle of the race. Unable to understand the Princess' attitude toward her suitors, both Aglante and Cynthie speak of the pleasures of love and urge her to consider her actions. The Princess declares that men act as slaves to women, only to become tyrants over them in the end, and that she will never succumb to the power of love. When told that even Diana, a goddess so admired by her, was not ashamed to show feelings of love, the Princess replies that human frailties have been erroneously attributed to the gods.

Moron arrives, and the cousins enlist his aid in their defense of love. They are interrupted by the arrival of Lycas, who announces that Iphitas, the Princess' father, is approaching, accompanied by the three princes. The Princess, alarmed, suspects that her father will oblige her to select one of them.

Anticipating her father's plan, the Princess quickly acknowledges the power of life and death which her lord has over her, declares her readiness to obey his command, and states that to give her a husband is to give her death. The Prince wishes only to see her married to one of these illustrious young Greeks, and he has offered a sacrifice to Venus, who seems to have promised a miracle. The loving father asks only that his daughter hide her coldness and agree to witness the race which is about to be held. Theocle and Aristomene are interested only in winning the heart of the Princess. Euryale shows his disdain for the Princess by saying that his only interest is in winning the race. Her pride hurt by this unexpected indifference, the Princess decides to witness the race. Later she will attempt to overcome Euryale's apparent disdain for her by professing a love for him. Cynthie warns of the dangers of such a game, but the Princess is confident that she can win it.

In an Interlude between Acts II and III, Moron tries unsuccessfully to court Philis, who cannot bear to listen to his unpleasant voice. He cannot sing and she will not let him talk. When he insists on talking, she runs away, leaving the unhappy lover to comment that the only way to win a woman is with music. A satyr offers to teach Moron to sing, but in the process they almost come to blows. The Interlude ends with dancing and gaiety.

ACT III.

Euryale has won the chariot race and in so doing has captured the admiration and the heart of the Princess. The latter, however, manages to hide her true feelings as she brings into play all her charms in an attempt to break down the resistance of this prince. Although he appears to be as insensitive as a rock to all the Princess' efforts to conquer him, Euryale has in fact fallen so completely in love with her that he can hardly resist throwing himself at her feet and confessing his great love for her. Moron advises him to be firm and to continue ignoring her.

The Princess approaches and Euryale, following Moron's advice, looks the other way. Moron hastens to speak alone with the Princess, who confesses that her burning desire now is to conquer this man's pride. Moron, playing both sides of the game, agrees that no one could be more deserving of such a fate. He warns her, however, that the prince is very hard and that he seems to have no interest in her whatsoever, since he has never spoken of her.

The Princess sends Moron to ask Euryale to come over and talk with her. Euryale insists that he cannot be persuaded to love anything. The Princess tries to trick him by saying that it is noble for a woman to appear insensitive to love, whereas a man must do homage to a woman of beauty and virtue if he does not wish to offend her. Euryale cannot see why a woman who herself will not give of her love can be so offended. The Princess replies that, though she does not care to love, she is glad to be loved. Euryale says that he does not wish to be loved, because

that would place obligations on him, and he does not wish
to appear ungrateful. His only love is liberty, and no woman, whatever her beauty and her charms, can win his love.

The Princess is more determined than ever to conquer the pride of this apparently insensitive man. She en-
lists the aid of Moron to speak for her and to try to get a
confession of love for her. When asked what she would do
then, she says that she would punish his disdain with coldness and all the cruelties she could imagine.

In an Interlude between Acts III and IV, Moron, who
has no talent for singing, competes for the love of his
Philis with a rival, Thyrsis, who sings beautifully. When
Moron, in his song, threatens to kill himself for love,
both Thyrsis and Philis encourage him to do that very
thing, the latter because she has never had a lover willing to die for her and she would like that.

ACT IV.

Using a new stratagem, the Princess confesses to
Euryale that she has had a change of heart, and that she
has decided to marry Aristomene, Prince of Messene.
Euryale congratulates her on her choice, and, fighting fire
with fire, declares that he has found Aglante to his liking
and will ask for her hand.

Foiled again in her campaign, the Princess is angered
that another could have succeeded where she has failed,
and she determines to thwart Euryale's plans. She first
tries unsuccessfully to persuade Aglante to refuse to accept Euryale. Later she tells Aristomene, who has heard
the good news from the lips of Euryale, that he must not
believe others in matters that concern her. When Moron
accuses the Princess of being like the dog in the manger,
and suggests that she really loves Euryale, he is summarily dismissed with dire threats to his well-being.

Alone, the Princess wonders whether it is possible that

indifference and disdain could have triumphed over respect and submission to break down her resistance to love. She calls for music to soothe her pain, and, in the Interlude which follows, Clymene and Philis sing a duet about love. The Princess does not wish to listen to the song, for it has only increased her anxiety, and she orders the singing stopped.

ACT V.

Euryale reveals to Iphitas his love for the Princess, and he explains the stratagem he has just used to try to force her to reveal her true feelings toward him. Iphitas promises Euryale the hand of his daughter, provided the latter shows that she loves him.

The Princess overhears her father agree to an alliance, and, thinking that he means a marriage with Aglante, she throws herself at the feet of Iphitas and begs him not to permit such a thing. She wishes to deny Euryale this pleasure because she hates him for the way in which he has scorned her. He should have courted her like the rest, so that she would at least have had the pleasure of refusing him. She will not permit him to be happy with Aglante, and she threatens to commit suicide if such an alliance takes place. Accused of being in love with Euryale, the Princess denies it vehemently, whereupon her father agrees that Euryale may not have Aglante and that, to prevent his ever having her, the Princess must take him for herself. When the Princess declares that Euryale does not wish that, the latter removes the mask and reveals his true feelings toward her. The Princess asks for a little time to think, and her implied acceptance leads Iphitas to offer Aglante and Cynthie to the two rejected princes.

In the Interlude which follows, shepherds and shepherdesses sing and dance in celebration of the Princess' engagement.

TARTUFFE; OR, THE IMPOSTOR

TARTUFFE; OR, THE IMPOSTOR
(TARTUFFE; OU, L'IMPOSTEUR)

CHARACTERS IN THE PLAY

ORGON: husband of Elmire.

DAMIS: his son.

VALERE: Mariane's lover.

CLEANTE: Orgon's brother-in-law.

TARTUFFE: a bigot.

M. LOYAL: a bailiff.

A POLICE OFFICER.

ELMIRE: Orgon's wife.

MADAME PERNELLE: Orgon's mother.

MARIANE: Orgon's daughter.

DORINE: her maid.

FLIPOTE: Madame Pernelle's maid.

The Scene is in Paris in Orgon's House.

ACT I.

The first act opens in the house of Orgon, where the sharp language of Madame Pernelle, the mother of Orgon, is very disagreeable to the other members of the household. These consist of Elmire, the young wife of Orgon, Cleante, brother of Elmire, Damis and Mariane, the children of Orgon, and the servant Dorine.

The subject under discussion is Tartuffe, a man who pretends to be very pious and who has become an inmate of the house of Orgon. Madame Pernelle believes in the piety of Tartuffe and takes exception to any remark made against him. When Orgon arrives home, he is informed that his wife has been ill, but he pays no attention to this news. Instead, he continually demands information about the health of Tartuffe. This very much disgusts Dorine.

Cleante, a man of good judgment, tries to show Orgon that Tartuffe is an impostor and a hypocrite; but he does not succeed in doing so, since Orgon is deaf to all reason. He replies to every argument with eulogies to the splendid and divine character of Tartuffe, who has so completely gained control over him.

ACT II.

Orgon has promised that his daughter shall marry her lover Valere. Unfortunately, at this point, Tartuffe also asks for the hand of Mariane; and in order not to disappoint such a holy person, Orgon breaks his word to Valere. This change of affairs does not appeal to Mariane. She protests to her father, but she argues in vain. Fortunately for her, however, she has the support of the quick-witted Dorine, who so disturbs Orgon by her arguments that he is finally driven to depart. "I must have a breath of air to compose myself," he says as he leaves.

A misunderstanding, which makes Valere believe that Mariane no longer loves him, fills up the remainder of the act. But due to the skillful manipulations of Dorine, the quarrel is reconciled and the lovers are reunited. They plan to make a common front against the proposed marriage of Tartuffe to Mariane.

ACT III.

The crowning scene of the third act is that in which Tartuffe makes a declaration of his love for Elmire, the wife of Orgon. Dorine, noticing that the hypocrite has been casting tender glances toward Elmire, advises her to lead him on to a proposal so that he can be unmasked.

Damis hides himself and listens to the conversation, which he reports to his father. Tartuffe, when confronted by his accusers, throws himself at the feet of Orgon. With subtle guile, in order to discredit Damis, he confesses that he is "a wicked, guilty, wretched sinner, full of iniquity, the greatest rogue that ever existed." Orgon is hoodwinked and turns with bitterness upon his son, who, he declares, should be punished for lying about such a holy man. He then insists that Tartuffe's marriage with Mariane shall take place that evening.

He disinherits Damis and tells Tartuffe that he is to be his heir. "A faithful and honest friend," he says, "is dearer to me than son, wife, and parents." Tartuffe pretends to dissuade Orgon from these decisions, but finally reluctantly yields. "The will of Heaven be done in all things," he says piously.

ACT IV.

However, Tartuffe is soon to be unmasked by Elmire. While Orgon lies hidden under a table, Elmire leads Tar-

Scene from Tartuffe.

tuffe to make love to her. He becomes very affectionate and uses many endearing terms. Finally he tells her that to sin in secret is not to sin at all and he hopes by means of this logic to make her unfaithful to her husband.

Elmire in her conversation compromises herself a little in order to unmask Tartuffe by leading the rascal on. When Orgon sees how matters stand, he reveals himself and faces the deceiver. Tartuffe, however, has another card to play, for he has in his possession some very valuable papers which belong to Orgon. One of these is the deed of gift to all his property. Another is a box of precious documents entrusted to him by an old friend, who has been forced to flee the country for some secret offense. The mere possession of these papers compromises Orgon and can be used against him.

ACT V.

Orgon now sees himself facing ruin on account of the viper whom he has cherished in his bosom, but his family is powerless to help him. His mother, Madame Pernelle, at first refuses to believe in the perfidy of Tartuffe until a bailiff appears upon the scene to arrest Orgon and to take possession of his goods in the name of Tartuffe.

While affairs are in this lamentable state, an officer arrives, who comes directly from the king himself. He states that he has been authorized to reestablish Orgon in the possession of his property, and also to arrest Tartuffe and take him to prison.

The king, explains the officer, is "an enemy of fraud," and in Tartuffe he has discovered a notorious rogue, whose life has been a long series of wicked acts.

Then joy reigns in the house of Orgon. Mariane marries Valere, and everything turns out happily.

DON JUAN

DON JUAN,

or The Feast of Stone

(DOM JUAN, ou Le Festin de Pierre)

CHARACTERS IN THE PLAY

DON JUAN: son of Don Louis.

SGANARELLE: Don Juan's valet.

ELVIRE: Don Juan's wife.

GUSMAN: servant of Elvire.

DON CARLOS: ⎫
　　　　　　 ⎬ brothers of Elvire.
DON ALONSE: ⎭

DON LOUIS: father of Don Juan.

FRANCISQUE: a beggar.

CHARLOTTE: ⎫
　　　　　　 ⎬ peasant girls.
MATHURINE: ⎭

PIERROT: a peasant.

THE STATUE OF THE COMMANDER.

LA VIOLETTE: ⎫
　　　　　　　⎬ lackeys of Don Juan.
RAGOTIN: ⎭

MONSIEUR DIMANCHE: a merchant.

LA RAMEE: an assassin.

The retinue of Don Juan.

A SPECTER

The scene is laid in Sicily. The first act is in a palace, with arcades and galleries open to walkers. The second act is at the edge of the sea. The third act is in a forest, within the trees of which is the tomb of the Commander. The fourth act is the apartment of Don Juan. The fifth act is a field near the city, then at the tomb.

ACT I.

Don Juan, a man devoid of all human emotions, except his debasing passion, has induced a girl named Elvire to leave the convent in which she lives and marry him. Becoming tired of his wife, Don Juan, on a flimsy pretext, departs suddenly to foreign parts so that he may have a clear field in which to remarry.

In the opening scene of the play, his servant, Sganarelle, learns that Elvire has come to the village in which Don Juan is then living. When Sganarelle informs his master of this fact, Don Juan coolly says that he has a new love and expresses his views on the subject of marriage in unmistakable terms. "All the pleasure of love is in change," he says. Expounding his thesis further, he finally exclaims: "I feel in me a desire to love all the world; and as Alexander, I wish that there were other worlds, so that I could extend my amorous conquests."

One wonders how Sganarelle could be faithful to such a master, but he reveals the truth to Gusman, the servant of Elvire. "Don Juan is the greatest rascal that the earth has ever produced," he says. But after enumerating his master's crimes, he concludes: "A great lord, who is an evil man, is a terrible thing; it is necessary that I be faithful to him, even though I hate him; my fear gives zeal to my services."

While Don Juan is outlining his views on marriage, his wife appears and tries to dissuade him from his evil life.

Don Juan tells her bluntly that he no longer cares for her and that their marriage, through its irregularity, was illegal. He then bids Sganarelle prepare to help him in an enterprise which he has devised to win a country girl from her lover.

ACT II.

The second act opens with a scene between Charlotte and Pierrot, two country lovers, in which the maid gives her promise to Pierrot that she will marry him.

In the meantime Don Juan and Sganarelle have attempted to carry out their amorous purposes, but their plot fails. They come upon Charlotte alone and Don Juan immediately makes love to her, receiving her promise to marry him in spite of a subsequent interruption from Pierrot.

Matherine, another girl to whom Don Juan has made love, appears on the scene and this considerably complicates matters; but the rogue succeeds in deceiving both of them.

Word then arrives through La Ramee that a band of a dozen men on horseback are in close pursuit of Don Juan. Their avowed purpose is to punish him for his misdeeds. The rascal attempts to persuade Sganarelle to change clothes with him, arguing that he is doing him an honor. "Happy is the valet," he says, "who has the glory of dying for his master." But Sganarelle declines the honor and they both flee.

ACT III.

Sganarelle, who clings to his master through all of his troubles, although, as he has already confessed, he hates his wicked ways, accompanies Don Juan disguised as a doctor. He tries to persuade his master to give up his evil life through fear of a vengeful heaven; but his words are unavailing.

As they proceed through the forest to which their flight has taken them, they are warned of robbers infesting the country. Shortly thereafter, Don Juan saves his wife's brother, Don Carlos, from death at the hands of the robbers. Don Carlos, who is unaware of the identity of his rescuer, reveals the fact that he and his brother, Don Alonse, have come to that part of the country with the express purpose of slaying Don Juan.

At that moment Don Alonse arrives. Recognizing Don Juan as the enemy whom he is seeking, he is about to attack the rogue, when Don Carlos intercedes and gets Don Juan reprieved for one day.

As Sganarelle and his master are leaving, they come upon a statue, which has been erected over the tomb of a general whom Don Juan had slain. Through a whim, Don Juan asks the statue to come to supper with him, and the statue nods acceptance.

ACT IV.

Don Juan, through his extravagant ways of living, is beset by creditors. Monsieur Dimanche, a merchant, who has been especially tenacious, arrives to collect the money owed him. Don Juan treats him like a long-lost friend, intercepting any attempt that the merchant makes to collect his bill. He speaks of him and his family in such endearing terms that the merchant is completely baffled.

Don Louis, the father of Don Juan, also arrives and attempts to lead his son into better paths; but Don Juan remains obdurate. Then his wife arrives, clad in a veil, to make the same appeal; but Don Juan is too hardhearted to listen to her.

Don Juan and his guests go to supper, but they have

scarcely commenced to eat, when the statue of the commander appears. All are terrified except the master, who
asks the commander to dine with him. The statue accepts
and, in its turn, it says to Don Juan: "I invite you to come
tomorrow and sup with me. Have you the courage?" Don
Juan accepts the invitation, saying that he will come accompanied by Sganarelle. But Sganarelle demurs, asserting that tomorrow is his day of fasting. Don Juan, however,
tells him to bring a torch; but the statue says that there
is no need for a light, when one is led by Heaven.

ACT V.

Apparently won over at last to a better way of living
by all the appeals made to him, Don Juan tells his father
that he has reformed. But upon the departure of Don Louis,
when Sganarelle is congratulating his master upon his
new resolution, he informs his servant that he has merely
become a hypocrite and does not mean what he says. Hypocrisy, he asserts, is a fashionable vice, and all fashionable vices pass as virtues. Moreover, hypocrisy has
marvelous advantages. "What a man! What a man!" says
poor Sganarelle sadly.

Don Carlos arrives, having heard of the apparent reform of his sister's husband and begs Don Juan to accept
Elvire as his wife and live with her. Don Juan hypocriti-
cally says that this is contrary to the mandates of heaven
which he has received.

At this point, a specter, clad in a veil, arrives and
tells Don Juan that he had better reform or that destruc-
tion will come upon him.

Don Juan defies the specter, whereupon the statue of
the commander comes and whirls him off to other regions
in the midst of thunder and lightning. The play ends with
the lamentations of Sganarelle for the loss of his wages.

THE LOVE DOCTOR

THE LOVE DOCTOR

(L'AMOUR MEDECIN)

CHARACTERS IN THE PLAY

SGANARELLE: father of Lucinde.

LUCINDE: daughter of Sganarelle.

CLITANDRE: lover of Lucinde.

AMINTE: neighbor of Sganarelle.

LUCRECE: niece of Sganarelle.

LISETTE: Lucinde's maid.

M. GUILLAUME: a seller of tapestries,

M. JOSSE: a goldsmith.

M. TOMES:

M. DES FONANDRES:

M. MACROTON: } physicians

M. BAHYS:

M. FILERIN:

A NOTARY

CHAMPAGNE: Sganarelle's valet.

The play is introduced with a "Prologue" given by three characters identified as Comedy, Music, and Ballet.

A Ballet is interspersed in three parts, the first by Champagne and four physicians, the second by a Quack accompanied by buffoons and Scaramouches, the third by Comedy, Music, and Ballet accompanied by characters called Sport, Laughter, and Pleasure.

The Scene is in Paris mainly in Sganarelle's House.

ACT I.

Lucinde, the daughter of Sganarelle, is ill and her father, fearing lest she should die, has called together several friends and relatives for a consultation. These people all give their opinions and suggest cures which appeal to their own fancies. Thus Josse, the goldsmith, suggests that Sganarelle should give his daughter a gift of diamonds, rubies, and emeralds. Guillaume asserts that a beautiful tapestry hung upon her wall would restore her. Aminte, a neighbor, suggests marriage, but Lucrece, the niece of Sganarelle, says that Lucinde is too ill to marry and that she should be placed in a convent.

Rejecting all of these suggestions, however, Sganarelle visits his daughter and tries to discover what the trouble is. Upon being asked whether she is in love, Lucinde nods. At this point, Lisette appears. She questions Lucinde and then informs Sganarelle that his daughter is in love, a fact which Sganarelle refuses to believe.

On account of her father's actions, Lucinde, with the help of Lisette, plans to deceive him. In pursuance of the plot, Lisette rushes into the room where Sganarelle is meditating and hints that Lucinde has been contemplating suicide. "She can no longer live with the displeasure of her father."

Much disturbed by this news, Sganarelle sends his valet to call in some physicians, who will tell him what the trouble is and how his daughter may be restored to health.

ACT II.

Lisette, who is represented as having unusually good sense, reproves her master for having called in four physicians. She quotes a man who said that a patient he once

knew did not die of a fever and an inflammation, but of
four physicians and two apothecaries.

The four physicians arrive, M. Tomes, M. Des Fonandres (Mankiller), M. Bahys (the Stutterer) and M. Macroton (the Slow Speaker).

Lisette, who recognizes Tomes, says that she had met
him at the home of Sganarelle's niece.

"How is her coachman feeling?" asks the physician.

"He is dead," replies Lisette.

"Impossible!" says Tomes. "Hippocrates says that
such a malady as his does not terminate for two or three
weeks, and he has been sick for only six days."

"Whatever Hippocrates says," replies Lisette. "The
coachman is dead and buried."

The physicians then dispute among themselves the val-
ues and the weaknesses of various schools of medicine.
The discussion is terminated by Tomes with the observation: "A man that's dead is only a dead man, and of no
special consequence; but a neglected formality carries a
notable injury throughout the entire body of physicians."

When the physicians finally get around to the case of
the sick Lucinde, they immediately differ in their diagno-
ses. Thomas says that she has a heating of the blood and
recommends bleeding. Fonandres, however, asserts that
she has a putrefaction of the humors and prescribes an
emetic. Bahys and Macroton, admonishing caution, appear
to agree that something is affecting her brain, but they
disagree as to just what this something is.

Poor Sganarelle, seeing the hopeless confusion of the
experts, then consults a charlatan and returns with a bottle of medicine, which is guaranteed to cure anything.

ACT III.

The third act opens with a discussion between the physicians M. Tomes, M. Des Fonandres, and M. Filerin on

the nature of their art. The latter, who has just arrived, points out that each profession is based upon some foible of mankind. The flatterer, he says, bases his art upon man's love of praise; the alchemist profits by pandering to man's love of riches; the astrologer casts his horoscopes to satisfy the vanity and flatter the ambition of the credulous. As for the physician, he makes his profits out of man's greatest foible, his love of life. "We sell our pompous nonsense through mankind's fear of death," says Filerin. The physicians then admonish each other to continue to deceive the people as to the true nature of the colossal fake which they represent.*

In the meantime, Clitandre, the lover of Lucinde, arrives on the scene clad in the garb of a physician. Lisette introduces him to Sganarelle as the exponent of a new kind of therapeutics, which treats diseases by means of words and mental suggestion. Sganarelle is very much pleased with this, and is greatly impressed when the new physician feels his pulse and is able to learn therefrom that Lucinde, his daughter, is ill. "This is due to the sympathy which exists between father and daughter," says the wily Clitandre.

Upon being introduced to Lucinde, Clitandre at once makes love and Sganarelle notices the immediate improvement in his daughter's health. Then Clitandre tells Sganarelle that his daughter is afflicted with the horrible disease of love. "By the science which Heaven has given me," says the physician, "I recognize that all her illness comes from her deranged imagination, from a depraved wish she has to be married. For myself, I see nothing

* In this interlude Molière shows his contempt for the medicine of the day, doubtless augmented by his own affliction of tuberculosis. Similar ridicule of physicians is found in much 17th and early 18th century literature, such, for example, as that of A. R. Lesage in *Gil Blas* (1715-35).

more foolish or ridiculous than this desire for marriage."

"What a great physician!" says Sganarelle.

Clitandre then suggests that Lucinde should be hu-
mored in her idea in order to effect a cure. Sganarelle
agrees and proposes that a marriage contract be made
out between the physician and Lucinde in order to delude
his daughter into believing that he desires to marry her.
Clitandre is quite willing and the two lovers depart immediately leaving the astonished father to meditate upon
the baseness of mankind.

THE MISANTHROPE

THE MISANTHROPE

(LE MISANTHROPE)

CHARACTERS IN THE PLAY

ALCESTE: lover of Celimene.

PHILINTE: friend of Alceste.

ORONTE: lover of Celimene.

CELIMENE: beloved by Alceste.

ELIANTE: cousin of Celimene.

ARSINOE: Celimene's friend.

ACASTE:
⎱ marquises.
CLITANDRE: ⎰

BASQUE: servant to Celimene.

DU BOIS: valet of Alceste.

AN OFFICER OF THE CONSTABULARY OF FRANCE.

The Scene is in Paris in Celimene's House.

ACT I.

Alceste, the misanthrope, and his friend, Philinte, expound their respective views on the frailty of mankind. Alceste's obsession is in the matter of sincerity. "I would that one should always be sincere," he says; "and if he be a man of honor, that he utter not one word that doesn't come from the heart." Since this is seldom practical and is not always followed by his friends, Alceste is intolerant and believes that all men should be shunned.

Philinte, on the other hand, is willing to pardon men's faults through compassion for their feebleness. "When one is in the world," he says, "it is necessary to conform to the civilities that custom demands." Philinte then gives Alceste some good advice. He informs him that he is in danger of losing an important lawsuit in which he is engaged, because of his rigidity in social intercourse. Philinte also warns him against bestowing his affections upon the coquette Celimene. "You are enchained by her, who only makes sport of you," he says, "while you neglect the sincere Eliante and the prudish Arsinoe, who both like you." But Alceste refuses to heed the advice of his friend.

At this point, Oronte, a rival for the affections of Celimene, arrives. He has come to read to Alceste some verses which he has just written. "I have composed a sonnet on 'Hope'," he says. It is obvious that he is seeking approval for his verses, although he confesses that he wrote the poem in a quarter of an hour. Although Philinte speaks kindly of the work, Alceste in no uncertain words calls it rubbish. He says that one should always use restraint in committing his thoughts to writing.

Oronte is very angry at the words of Alceste and a lively duel of mutual recriminations results, which is stopped only with effort by Philinte. Oronte then departs in a rage.

ACT II.

The second act opens with a conversation between Alceste and Celimene in which the former asks Celimene to end her numerous flirtations. Two marquises arrive, Acaste and Clitandre, who are both in love with Celimene. She also receives other visitors in the persons of Philinte and her cousin, Eliante, who is as sincere as Celimene is artificial.

In the lively conversation which ensues Celimene makes sport of many types of people seen in society. One of these she describes as "A great talker, who manages to tell you nothing with a long flow of words." Another makes mysteries out of the insignificant, creating mountains out of molehills, all of which he conveys into one's ear by means of whispers. A third she characterizes as a name-dropper, who "never quotes anyone lower in rank than a Duke, a Prince, or a Princess." About another she states that he is always laboring to create witty sayings; "and since he wants to be clever, nothing suits him." Even her lady friends receive the benefit of her sharp tongue. Belise, she says, has exhausted her conversation as soon as she has finished with the various aspects of the weather.

Alceste chides Celimene, not because she sees the weakness in her friends, but because of her hypocrisy when they are present. "Let one of them appear," he says, "and you will rush out to meet that one with a flattering kiss and protestations of friendship.

Philinte in his turn reproves Alceste for his critical attitude toward mankind, but fails to understand how he can love Celimene with all her faults. Alceste admits the charge, but defends himself by saying that he constantly points out these shortcomings to her. "The more we are in love with anyone," he says, "the less we should flatter her. True love reveals itself by excusing nothing."

The scene ends with the arrival of a mandate to Alceste from the Tribunal of the Marshals of France in the matter of the affair of honor which arose out of the altercation with Oronte. He is asked to appear before the Tribunal. But he defies them with the statement: "Unless there is an express order from the King himself commanding me to approve the verses which have caused all the trouble, I shall always maintain, by Jove, that they are bad and that the man who made them deserves hanging."

ACT III.

The marquises, Acaste and Clitandre, discuss together their affair with Celimene and decide to ask her to make a confession of love for one of them. They admit that their progress with her has been slow, but they agree that the one who can show positive proof of her affection for him will be given a free field by the other.

Before they can test the matter, however, the prude Arsinoe arrives and they depart. Although Celimene has just disparaged her to the marquises, she greets Arsinoe with hypocritical affection. Arsinoe tells Celimene that terrible whispers are going around about her. But Celimene receives this news with indifference and retaliates by relating gossip which she has heard about her guest. Arsinoe is much disturbed by these remarks and decides to have revenge by sharing with Alceste her proofs of Celimene's perfidy.

As Celimene excuses herself to write a letter, Alceste arrives and Arsinoe makes full use of this opportunity to carry out her designs. After first attempting to flatter him — an effort which he derides with his usual contempt for the opinions of the world — she tells him that she has proof of Celimene's betrayal of his affections. Alceste expresses interest but says: "With respect to such a revelation, doubts are the most distressing; what I desire for myself is that which reveals with clarity the truth of what is told me." "Accompany me to my house," replies Arsinoe, "and I will give you the proof you desire."

ACT IV.

The scene opens with a conversation between Philinte and Eliante in which the former describes what happened in the conference between Alceste and Oronte before the Tribunal of Marshals. Although Alceste refused to retract, he admitted that a man may still be a gentleman and yet write bad verses. He argued, therefore, that such a situation has nothing to do with honor. The matter was finally settled amicably when Alceste consented to phrase his criticism in gentler terms, and the rivals settled their dispute with an embrace.

Eliante confesses an affection for Alceste. To this Philinte responds with doubts about the consummation of the match between her cousin and the misanthrope. He then expresses his own hope that he may be wrong in this judgment, so that Eliante may then, perhaps, transfer her affection to him.

Alceste arrives very much disturbed by the proof which Arsinoe has given him of the perfidy of Celimene. This was in the form of a letter written by her allegedly to Oronte, in which she expressed her love for his rival. In his distress Alceste is about to offer his hand to Eliante, when Celimene arrives. Under her caresses and soft words his fury abates and he is almost deluded into the belief that the letter was not written to Oronte, but to one of her women friends.

He is still somewhat undecided and is on the point of demanding a better proof than Celimene has furnished him, when Dubois, his valet, interrupts the conversation with bad news. A legal document has just been presented to him from the lawyer who is opposing A l c e s t e in the impending suit about which Philinte previously had given him some advice.

Celimene then dismisses Alceste with the words: "Do not fly into a passion with me, but hasten to unravel this embarrassment of your own." To this Alceste replies that he will resume the conversation with her later.

ACT V.

Alceste loses his l a w s u i t, which makes him more bitter than ever toward the human race. He resolves to withdraw from the world into a place where he may dwell alone. His friend Philinte attempts to dissuade him and advances the proposition that "if everyone were clothed in probity, and if all hearts were frank, just, and docile, then the greater part of our virtues would be useless, since we need them only to help us bear without vexation the injustice of others in our rightful cause." But Alceste rejects this philosophy and asks to be let alone until he has probed the love of Celimene.

Oronte arrives with Celimene. Not noticing at first that Alceste is in the room, he urges her to accept his suit instead of that of the misanthrope. Thereupon Alceste makes himself known and warmly urges the lady to choose between them. While this argument is in progress, Eliante, Philinte, Arsinoe, and the two marquises, Acaste and Clitandre, appear. The battle over Celimene then becomes general. Arsinoe states that the two marquises have just consulted her about letters which they had individually received from Celimene. The two letters are read and are found to be devastating in the scathing criticism which they contain about each one of Celimene's four suitors. Celemine, thus unmasked, is speechless. Oronte and the two marquises depart in a rage.

Since the heart of Alceste now seems to be free, Arsinoe hints that she might be an easy conquest to replace
his lost love. But Alceste undeceives her by stating that
if he ever sought revenge by choosing another love, Arsinoe would never be that one.

Celimene, in confusion, then confesses to Alceste her
wantonness, but says that her criticism of him did not
come from her heart. Although she despised the others,
she states that this is not true with respect to Alceste.
Since he still loves Celimene, in spite of her treachery,
he makes her a proposition. If she will follow him into the
wilderness where he is going, then he will forgive her
duplicity. But Celimene, stating that such a solitude to a
young woman is frightful to contemplate, refuses to go.
Then Alceste's love turns to hatred and he scornfully denounces her.

The play ends with a statement by Alceste of his high
regard for the sincerity of Eliante, in contrast to that of
her cousin. She in her turn tells Philinte that if he should
ask for her hand, she would probably accept him.

THE PHYSICIAN IN SPITE OF HIMSELF

THE PHYSICIAN IN SPITE OF HIMSELF

(LE MEDECIN MALGRE LUI)

CHARACTERS IN THE PLAY

SGANARELLE: husband of Martine.

MARTINE: wife of Sganarelle.

M. ROBERT: a neighbor of Sganarelle.

VALERE: servant of Geronte.

LUCAS: husband of Jacqueline.

GERONTE: father of Lucinde.

JACQUELINE: nurse at Geronte's house, wife of Lucas.

LUCINDE: daughter of Geronte.

LEANDRE: lover of Lucinde.

THIBAUT: a peasant, father of Perrin.

PERRIN: a peasant, son of Thibaut.

In the first act the scene is a clearing in the forest near the house of Sganarelle. In the second act the scene represents a room in Geronte's house. The opening scene in the third act is a spot near Geronte's house; in the third scene we return to a room in Geronte's house.

ACT I.

The play opens with an entertaining and quite spirited scene of domestic infelicity. Martine, the wife of Sganarelle, is reproving her husband for his general worthlessness, which consists principally of a congenital inaptitude for work and an extreme fondness for the joys of the bottle. Sganarelle attempts to defend himself by asking his spouse whether she knows another binder of faggots, who can argue as well as he and who has had the honor of serving a famous physician for six years. These qualities only increase her scorn. Sganarelle finally loses his temper and, asserting his lordship over his own house, he proceeds to beat his wife.

The ensuing cries of help from Martine bring a neighbor, M. Robert, to the scene of conflict. But when Robert attempts to interfere in the quarrel, Martine sides with her husband. She asserts that he has the right to beat her if he wishes without any interference from an outsider. Sganarelle tells Robert to remember the wise saying of Cicero: "Beware about placing your finger between the tree and its bark." Driving Robert away, he returns to his wife and suggests that they reconcile their differences. This she grudgingly agrees to do, but, communing with herself, she confesses that she awaits a chance to be avenged.

This opportunity soon presents itself, when, by accident, Martine overhears a conversation between Valere and Lucas, members of the household of Squire Geronte. They are searching for a physician who can cure Geronte's daughter of a malady that has deprived her of speech. Martine informs them that there lives near at hand a very famous physician, Sganarelle by name, but that he will never admit his skill nor give aid unless he is forced to do so. She relates some of the marvelous cures that he has made. "You will find him in that little place yonder, where, to amuse himself, he is cutting wood," she says. "He is a very eccentric, fantastic sort of a man, who conceals his art by pretending ignorance of it." At times, she asserts, he is so mad that there is only one way to make him admit his profession. "He must be beaten with sticks until he confesses what he is."

"What a strange delusion," says Valere. But he and Lucas are finally persuaded by the wonderful case histories which Martine relates to them. She says that Sganarelle is easily recognized, since he has a large black beard and wears a ruff and a yellow and green coat.

Shortly thereafter the two men come upon Sganarelle, who is much amazed by their actions. He denies vigorously that he is a physician, but they proceed to subdue him by beating him with clubs. Sganarelle finally agrees with them. "Yes, I am a physician," he says, "and an apothecary as well, or anything else you like if you will just stop the blows." When they inform him that he will be well paid for his efforts, his objections to being a physician vanish and he agrees to go with them to Geronte's house provided they will furnish him with a physician's gown.

ACT II.

Valere and Lucas are much elated over their find and boast that they have brought with them the best physician in the world. Lucas admits, however, that he seems at times a little cracked. Jacqueline, the nurse, Lucas' wife, says that no physician can help Lucinde. She is in love with Leandre, she asserts, but her father is forcing her to marry Holdfast, since he is wealthy. Although Leandre has expectations of inheriting his uncle's estate, Geronte believes that a bird-in-hand is better than one in the bush; or as he picturesquely expresses it: "While the grass grows the cow starves.'' In the meantime Lucinde remains mute.

Upon being introduced into the house of Geronte, Sganarelle meets the master, whom he mistakes for a fellow physician. But when Geronte informs him to the contrary, Sganarelle begins to beat him with a stick, saying that such an initiation is all that is necessary to become a physician. "I have never taken any other degree," he says.

Sganarelle finds Jacqueline much to his liking and begins to make love to her until Lucas interferes with some display of heat. Later Sganarelle renews his suit by prescribing remedies for her imaginary ills, but these she rejects stating that she will not have her body used as an apothecary's shop.

The fake physician finally sees Lucinde, the mute girl, and discourses wisely upon her condition. After due consideration of her case, he says that he has discovered that her trouble is merely that she is without the power of speech. By a great display of garbled phrases and false words, Sganarelle makes Geronte believe that he is well informed in medicine in spite of such little inaccuracies as placing the heart and the liver on the wrong side of the body. This discrepancy Sganarelle explains by stating that physicians today are practicing medicine on an entirely new system.

Upon leaving the house Sganarelle meets Leandre, who informs him that Lucinde is only pretending to be mute so that she will not have to marry a person whom she does not love. When Leandre gives him a purse, Sganarelle agrees to help him in his love affair.

ACT III.

In the third act, Sganarelle, accompanied by Leandre, who is now dressed in the garb of an apothecary, appears

at the house of Geronte to see his patient. Sganarelle renews his proposals of love to the nurse Jacqueline, who
does not spurn them. She accepts his unflattering description of her husband without argument. "It is a penance
for my sins," she says, "but where the goat is tied down,
there she must browse." Unfortunately for the burgeoning
romance, however, Lucas is concealed in the room. Just
as they are about to embrace he rushes between them and
they separate in much confusion.

Sganarelle and Leandre then go to see Lucinde. While
the two lovers are talking, the false physician attracts
Geronte's attention in another direction. Suddenly, however, Geronte becomes aware that his daughter has re-
gained the power of speech and he is overcome with gratitude to Sganarelle who has achieved this cure.

But the first words of Lucinde disconcert her father,
for she vows that she will marry Leandre and no other.
Geronte replies that he will never have Leandre for a
son-in-law. Sganarelle then turns to his apothecary and
tells him that it is necessary to give Lucinde some medicine immediately to cure her of this love. He orders him
to leave at once and prepare it. Leandre takes the hint
and the two lovers elope under the very nose of the father.

Martine, who has been searching for her husband, finds
him at last at the house of Geronte. She is informed that
he is about to be hanged because of his treachery to Geronte. This news does not appear to disturb her very much,
for she requests permission to remain to see the hanging.

At this dramatic moment Leandre and Lucinde return
after having been married. The wrath of Geronte is soon
appeased, however, when Leandre informs him that he has
just become wealthy by the opportune demise of his rich
uncle. Sganarelle forgives his wife for the trick she has
played upon him because "he has now become a man of
consequence."

MELICERTE

MELICERTE

CHARACTERS IN THE PLAY

ACANTE: lover of Daphne.

TYRENE: lover of Eroxene.

DAPHNE: a shepherdess.

EROXENE: a shepherdess.

LYCARSIS: a shepherd, believed to be the father of Myrtil.

MYRTIL: lover of Melicerte.

MELICERTE: nymph or shepherdess, beloved by Myrtil.

CORINNE: confidante of Melicerte.

NICANDRE: a shepherd.

MOPSE: a shepherd, believed to be the uncle of Melicerte.

The Scene is in Thessaly in the Vale of Tempe.

Melicerte is a historic pastoral, which was never completed, only two acts being written. In 1699 the son of the
comedian Guerin, who had married Moliere's widow, wrote
a terminal third act, which does not appear to have sur-
vived. The play was given first on December 2, 1666 in
the Ballet of the Muses held at Saint-Germain, but was
soon replaced by the Comic Pastoral.

ACT I.

Daphne and Eroxene, two shepherdesses are beloved
respectively by the shepherds, Acante and Tyrene, but
they do not return this love since they are charmed by
another. As soon as their rejected lovers have departed,
they reveal to each other the name of the new flame, who
happens to be the same for both of them, namely, Myrtil.

In order to solve their problem, the two girls seek
the advice of Lycarsis, the supposed father of Myrtil, and
he promises that he will persuade his son to marry one
of them. But when the proposition of choosing one of the
girls for his wife is presented to Myrtil, he tells them
that he has given his heart to Melicerte. This greatly
enrages his father.

ACT II.

The second act reveals the character of the gentle
Melicerte, nymph or shepherdess, in a conversation with
her lover, Myrtil. Lycarsis arrives and by his harsh
words so disturbs the young lady that she bids farewell
to her lover and flees. Myrtil then makes a strong appeal
to his father in behalf of Melicerte and finally wins his
consent to his marriage with her.

This has just been accomplished and they are about to
depart to break the news to Mopse, a shepherd believed

to be the uncle of Melicerte, when word arrives that the king of the country, who has just made a visit to that section, has carried her away. He intends to make Melicerte the wife of one of his great lords for she is of noble blood. The act ends with the lamentations of Myrtil over his hard fate.

THE COMIC PASTORAL

THE COMIC PASTORAL
(PASTORALE COMIQUE)

CHARACTERS IN THE PLAY

IRIS: a young shepherdess.

LYCAS: a rich shepherd.

FILENE: a rich shepherd.

CORIDON: a young shepherd.

A PLAYFUL SHEPHERD

A SHEPHERD

The Comic Pastoral is a light musical comedy, the slender plot of which is based upon the unrequited love of the rich shepherds Lycas and Filene for Iris. The two lovers are wandering in the forest when each hears the other pronounce the name of Iris. This arouses their anger and they begin to fight.

A band of shepherds rushes upon the scene to separate the two men, but the members of the band fall to quarreling among themselves. It is now left to the young shepherd, Coridon, to bring peace out of the melee, and he is rewarded for his efforts by receiving the love of Iris.

Jilted in this fashion, Lycas and Filene meditate death. But they are counseled to abandon such an idea by a young shepherd, who shows them the folly of such grief over a lost love.

The choruses of magicians, demons, and Egyptians are pretty bits of lyric verse, and furnish a pleasing color to the comedy.

Jean-Baptiste Lully,
who provided the music for a number of Molière's plays including
The Sicilian.

THE SICILIAN, OR THE AMOROUS PAINTER

THE SICILIAN, OR THE AMOROUS PAINTER

(LE SICILIEN, OU L'AMOUR PEINTRE)

CHARACTERS IN THE PLAY

ADRASTE: a French gentleman, lover of Isidore.

DON PEDRE: a Sicilian, lover of Isidore.

ISIDORE: a Greek slave belonging to Don Pedre.

CLIMENE: sister of Adraste.

HALI: valet of Adraste.

THE SENATOR

MUSICIANS

A TROOP OF SLAVES

A TROOP OF MOORS

TWO LACKEYS

The Scene is principally a Public Place near the house of Don Pedre.

This one act play opens with a serenade given before the house of Don Pedre, a Sicilian nobleman. The entertainment has been arranged by Adraste, a young Frenchman, who has fallen in love with Isidore, a beautiful Greek girl, who dwells therein. But his suit has been thwarted by Don Pedre, since Isidore is his slave, and since, moreover, he himself is in love with her and guards her with great jealousy.

Adraste explains his difficulty to Hali, his valet. "It is true that we have often spoken to one another with our eyes," he says, "but it is now necessary that we explain our love, each to the other, by means of words." The accomplishment of this, however, has presented obvious difficulties.

While the musicians are singing, Don Pedre appears in his night clothes, with a sword under his arm, to learn both the reason for the serenade and the identity of its instigators. The Don, concealing himself from the serenaders, soon discovers that Adraste is in love with his "lovely Grecian" and that he plots mischief against "that traitor of a Sicilian" who guards her. At this point Hali observes that the door of the house is open, but when he attempts to enter, the Don gives him a slap on the cheek, an insult which Hali promptly returns. Thereupon the Don, breathing fire, shouts for his servants, his shield, his pistols, his muskets, and his guns, declaring that no quarter will be given. This promptly ends the serenade.

The next morning Don Pedre awakens the beautiful Isidore before she has completed her beauty sleep.

"Why so early?" she asks.

"I have some business that obliges me to leave at this hour," replies the Don, "and I wish to have you with me. It is not a bad idea to insure oneself a little against the cares of watchfulness. Indeed, last night there was singing under our windows."

"It was adorable," says Isidore.

"Was it for you?" asks the Don.

"I hope so," replies Isidore.

Thereupon the Don confesses that he is in love with his beautiful slave and that he wishes to marry her despite the fact that he is her master. But she replies that marriage would only change her status from one kind of slavery into another, since he would still not grant her freedom. The Don protests that he does this only through his excessive love for her.

"If that is your idea of love," replies Isidore, "I pray you to hate me instead."

The first stratagem introduced to gain access to Isidore is made by Hali, who appears at Don Pedre's house with a troupe of musicians. These he introduces to the Don as slaves for whom he is seeking a master, and suggests that perhaps the wealthy Sicilian might wish to purchase them after he has seen them perform.

Directing their attention especially to Isidore, the musicians dance, while Hali chants a song. In this he reveals that a certain person is in love with a beautiful lady, but that he is restrained from declaring his love by an odious and jealous master. Thus far, chants the wily Hali, he has been able to convey his message only with his eyes. Don Pedre, however, sees through the scheme and drives Hali and his dancers from the house.

When the valet reports his lack of success to Adraste, the latter says that he has devised a stratagem which should succeed. For this purpose he appears at the home of Don Pedre with a letter introducing him as Francois, a famous French artist, who is to take the place of his friend Damon, originally commissioned to paint a picture of Isidore. "Don't speak to him of any payment," writes Damon. "This would offend him, since he works only for glory and reputation."

The Don is very much pleased to learn this, but he is not so happy when Francois salutes Isidore with a kiss. "It is the French method of greeting," explains the painter, to which Don Pedre replies tartly that it is not the method in vogue in his country. Although the Don watches the proceedings with the eyes of an eagle, Adraste in various ways, by means of compliments and the arrangement of appropriate poses for his model, succeeds in conveying his message to Isidore.

While this masque is in progress, Hali appears, dressed as a Spaniard. Introducing himself as Don Gilles d'Avalos, he tells Don Pedre that he was recently insulted by receiving a slap on his cheek and that he is seeking advice as to what he should do to the one who had thus mistreated him.

"Should I thrash the man or have him assassinated?" asks the wily Hali.

While the attention of the Don is thus diverted, Adraste continues his lovemaking, which is properly received by Isidore.

After Adraste has departed, and while the Don is questioning Isidore about Francois, Climene, the sister of Adraste, her features concealed by a veil, comes running to meet them. She begs their protection from an irate and jealous husband, who is pursuing her with a sword.* The Don agrees to assist her and tells her to withdraw into the house with Isidore, where she will be safe.

As they leave, Adraste arrives and pretends, in the role of Francois, that he is the pursuing husband. "Let me treat the traitor as she deserves" he asks the Don.

But Don Pedre replies that he believes the wife's fault is much too small to generate such wrath in her husband. After some debate on the matter, the Don finally persuades

* In the original play, the role of the petitioner was not Climene, but Zaide, a young slave, whom her master had cruelly mistreated.

Adraste to cool his anger and become reconciled with his wife. As soon as this is settled, Isidore, concealed under the veil of Climene, appears and is handed over to Adraste by the Don, who says to him: "For the love of me, I conjure you to live in a perfect union together."

"For the love of you," replies Adraste, "I promise to do exactly that."

But when Don Pedre, having thus settled the matter so nicely, calls for Isidore, Climene appears, without her veil, and reveals the sad truth to him that his charming Greek slave has departed with her lover. The Don cries for justice, but when he appeals to the Senator, who acts in the capacity of a judge, he receives cold comfort and is told to take his troubles to the devil.

L'AVARE

AMPHITRYON

AMPHITRYON

CHARACTERS IN THE PLAY

MERCURY

NIGHT

JUPITER: under the form of Amphitryon.

AMPHITRYON: general of the Thebans.

ALCMENE: the wife of Amphitryon.

CLEANTHIS: maid of Alcmene and wife of Sosie.

SOSIE: Amphitryon's valet.

ARGATIPHONITIDAS:

NAUCRATES:
} captains of the Thebans.

POLIDAS:

POSICLES:

The Scene is in Thebes before the House of Amphitryon.

The play of Amphitryon is an adaptation by Moliere
of the classical comedy produced by the Roman dramatist Plautus (254-184 B. C.) It opens with a prologue in
which Mercury prevails upon Night to slow up her chariot,
since Jupiter is with Alcmene, the wife of Amphitryon, a
Theban general, whose form he has assumed. Mercury
then bids farewell to Night, telling her that he is about
to descend to the earth, where he will assume the form
of Amphitryon's valet, Sosie.

ACT I.

In the first scene we encounter the real Sosie. Carrying a lantern, for it is dark, he has been sent ahead by his
master to announce his return to Thebes. While Sosie in
a long soliloquy is rehearsing what he will tell Alcmene
about the glories of the general's victory, he notices that
the night seems unusually long and hazards the guess that
Phoebus may have overslept from having indulged in too
much wine. While thus bemused he encounters Mercury,
who, in his image, has just departed from Amphitryon's
house. A lively dialogue ensues in which Mercury prevents Sosie from entering the house with several well-
directed blows from a club.
    When Mercury asks Sosie his name and receives the
reply that it is Sosie and that he is the valet of Amphitryon, Mercury denies this and claims both the name and
the position as his own. In order to enforce his assertions, he beats Sosie until the poor fellow is completely
bewildered. When Mercury repeats his question as to his
name, Sosie replies: "Up to now I have believed that I was
Sosie, but your beating has finally convinced me that I
have been mistaken."
    In the course of the conversation, poor Sosie's be-
wilderment increases when his *alter ego* is able to de-

scribe the gift which Amphitryon is bringing to Alcmene, a cluster of five large diamonds contained in a sealed casket. As they approach Amphitryon's house, Mercury refuses to let Sosie enter and drives him off with blows of his club. As the poor valet departs to return to his master, he laments: "What a 'wonderful' ambassador I have made!"

In the final scene of this act Jupiter takes leave of Alcmene, who, believing that she has spent the night with Amphitryon, expresses her great pleasure in being a part of his victories and in sharing his love. They are accompanied by Mercury and Cleanthis, the latter the servant of Alcmene and the wife of Sosie. But Mercury expresses no love for her, and she, thinking that he is Sosie, is much upset by his indifference, especially after a reunion so long delayed. As Mercury leaves to join his master, she vows vengeance upon the wretch.

ACT II.

Sosie returns to Amphitryon and reports that he has not been successful in delivering his message to Alcmene. His master, much disturbed by this, makes a searching enquiry into the reasons; but Sosie, himself completely confused, cannot make Amphitryon understand that there are two Sosies.

"Must I repeat the same thing to you twenty times," says the poor valet. "This I, I tell you, is stronger than I am; this I secured the door by force; this I made me knuckle under to him, and wished to be the only I; this I has broken me with blows."

"His brain is addled; he has been drinking too much," Amphitryon decides.

While they are talking, Alcmene and Cleanthis appear, and Amphitryon hastens to greet them. But to his astonishment his wife, instead of showing the expected raptures at seeing her husband, exclaims: "What is this? Why do you return so soon?"

The inevitable misunderstanding occurs, which soon develops into mutual recriminations, since Amphitryon, like poor Sosie, is unable to comprehend that he is the victim of two identities. The mystery deepens when Alcmene, to prove that her husband has already visited her, says that she has in her possession the cluster of diamonds which he had given her.

"What? That I have already given you!" exclaims the bewildered Amphitryon.

"She makes sport of you," says Sosie. "I have them here."

But when the casket is opened it is found to be empty, which only increases the mystery and does nothing to allay the suspicion of the general that he is the victim of double dealing. When Amphytrion appeals to Sosie for an explanation of his wife's behavior, the valet says: "She is in need of six grains of hellebore; her mind is twisted." By this statement he conveys his belief that she is mentally deranged, since this drug was thought in those days to alleviate insanity.

Finally Amphitryon departs in a jealous rage saying that he will return with Alcmene's brother as a witness that he has never been near his house until that morning.

After the departure of husband and wife, the marital problems of Sosie and Cleanthis again present themselves. As in the previous discussion, no solution is found. When Sosie suggests that they forget their terrible fracus, Cleanthis replies: "What good is that? Let us send all men to the devil, for the best of them is worth nothing."

ACT III.

In the first scene poor baffled Amphitryon, again ar-

arriving at his house, is denied admission by Mercury, who pretends not to know him and addresses him in the most insolent language. Finally Mercury orders him to depart, since he appears to have drunk too much wine. Moreover, says the sly rogue, he must not disturb Amphitryon, who is within enjoying his return home from his victories and all the pleasures that attend the reunion with his wife.

While the bewildered general is fulminating and vowing vengeance upon his insolent servant, Sosie appears with Naucrates and Polidas, two of his captains. When Amphitryon would assault Sosie, the captains intervene and tell him that they have just been invited by the valet to have dinner with him.

"Who gave this order?" shouts Amphitryon.

"You," replies Sosie, "after you had appeased the wrath of Alcmene."

"Oh, Heavens!" cries Amphitryon; "each step adds something else to my cruel fate."

While this uproar is going on, Jupiter appears and now there is real confusion.

"What prodigy is this?" cries Naucrates. "Here are two Amphitryons."

Amphitryon, beside himself with rage, berates Jupiter as an impostor, a judgment concurred in by Sosie, who says that he should be chastised.

"Such execrable knavery is too much to be endured," shouts Amphitryon. "It is necessary to break this enchantment with iron."

But Naucrates intervenes, and, when Jupiter says that his *alter ego* is so beside himself with rage that he has lost his reason, the captain decides that he will not permit such a strange combat as Amphitryon fighting himself.

A lengthy debate then ensues as to which is the true Amphitryon. Jupiter then suggests that the Thebans, who know the general well, must decide between them and that this can best be done by attending a banquet which has been prepared for them. It is at this point that Sosie makes his famous judgment, which is frequently quoted: "The real Amphitryon is the one who gives dinners."

This remark, however, further enrages the general, who swears that he will have his revenge upon the impostor even though he must follow him to hell.

"That will not be necessary," says Jupiter, "for you will soon see that I shall not flee from you."

"This entire adventure confounds one's sense and reason," is the judgment of Naucrates.

"Well, let us dine," says Sosie. "Never have I been so hungry."

As the group leaves to attend the banquet, Mercury appears and detains Sosie. The poor valet still attempts, but in vain, to assert his identity.

"Let there be two Sosies, just as there are two Amphitryons," he begs.

"No," replies Mercury. "There must be only one."

"I will be the younger, and you the older," says Sosie.

When Mercury forbids this also, the poor valet cries: "Then let me be your shadow."

"Not even that," replies Mercury.

While they are arguing, Amphitryon appears in company with his two captains Argatiphonitidas and Posicles, who are also unable to unravel the mystery. Sosie complains of his bitter fate and says that he has been "de-Sosied," just as his master has been "de-Amphitryoned."

The confusion is increased when Cleanthis and Naucrates appear. "Good heavens!" cries Cleanthis when she sees the general. "What is the matter with you?" asks the general. "Do I inspire you with fear?"

"You are upstairs and yet you are here," cries the bewildered Cleanthis.

But the mystery is soon to be resolved, for at that moment Mercury appears and states that all is caused by the king of the gods, who has come in the form of Amphitryon to visit Alcmene. Mercury appeases Sosie also by revealing his true identity and telling him that he should feel honored by having been beaten by a god.

"In faith! Monsieur god, I am your valet," says Sosie, "and I am satisfied by your courtesy."

"Well, I must be going back to heaven," says Mercury, "where I can cleanse myself with some ambrosia."

Jupiter now appears on a cloud and consoles Amphitryon with the statement that to share a wife with a god is by no means dishonorable. He also adds that soon a son is to be born, who will be Hercules, a hero who will fill the universe with his deeds.

The final philosophy of the play is brought out by Sosie, who declares that under such circumstances as these the best thing is to say nothing.

GEORGE DANDIN

GEORGE DANDIN

CHARACTERS IN THE PLAY

GEORGE DANDIN: a rich peasant, husband of Angelique.

ANGELIQUE: wife of George Dandin and daughter of M. de Sotenville.

M. DE SOTENVILLE: nobleman, father of Angelique.

MADAME DE SOTENVILLE: his wife.

CLITANDRE: enamored of Angelique.

CLAUDINE: servant of Angelique.

LUBIN: peasant, servant of Clitandre.

COLIN: valet of George Dandin.

The Scene is in front of the house of George Dandin.

ACT I.

This amusing comedy is the dramatization of the plot of the sixty-fourth story in the *Decameron* of Boccaccio. The play opens with a soliloquy by George Dandin, a man who does not belong to the nobility, but who has a fair sized fortune. He has married above his station, his wife Angelique being the daughter of a poor nobleman, M. de Sotenville. In the soliloquy Dandin bemoans his fate, lamenting that it was his wealth and not himself that was married.

Although his father-in-law receives pecuniary help from him, the noble and his wife heap all kinds of indignities upon poor Dandin, constantly reminding him of the honor which has been bestowed upon him by the marriage. This soliloquy has been compared with the similar reflections of Strepsiades in *The Clouds* of Aristophanes. In that play, the hero, a lover of country life, in like manner had sold himself in marriage to a haughty lady of the town.

Through a mistake in identity, Lubin, the bumbling servant of Clitandre, reveals to Dandin that his master is having an affair with Angelique. Dandin in a rage confronts M. de Sotenville and his wife with the unpleasant news, but they are unwilling to believe it. Dandin then confronts them with Clitandre, who not only denies everything, but asks for satisfaction for such an accusation. Angelique is then brought into the matter and, supported by Claudine, her maid, makes a spirited defense.

Since Dandin does not possess the evidence to support his accusations, his father-in-law insists that he must apologize to Clitandre, and must conclude with the words: "I am your servant." Dandin is aghast at this and protests that he should not be forced to say that he is a servant of one who has had an affair with his wife. However, he is finally persuaded to make the admission.

The act concludes with another soliloquy: "Ah that I — You would have it so, you would have it so, George Dandin, you would have it so! This suits you very well, and you must adjust to it. You have exactly what you deserve." But he is not yet reconciled to his fate and decides that he will find some means to prove his point.

ACT II.

Emboldened by the success which they have had in deceiving her parents, Angelique and Clitandre continue their relations. Finally, however, Dandin believes that he has a chance to expose his wife. He discovers her having an amorous conversation with her lover. Whereupon, desiring to present this evidence to his parents-in-law, he leads them to the place where they may overhear what is being said.

Unfortunately for his plans, however, Angelique sees them coming and she pretends to be very angry with Clitandre for having made dishonorable proposals to her. Poor Dandin is again left without any foundations for his assertions and is forced once more to apologize.

ACT III.

Angelique and Clitandre are having a rendezvous one night, when they are surprised by George Dandin, who closes the house door so that Angelique cannot get in again. Now, at last, he is in a position to expose the unfaithfulness of his wife. Thereupon he sends his valet, Colin, to summon his parents-in-law in order that they may have full proof. While things are in this state, Angelique pretends to be dying of despair.

"If you reduce me to desperation," she says, "I assure you that a lady in my extremity is capable of anything and I will do that of which you will repent."

"Please tell me what you propose to do," replies the skeptical Dandin.

"My heart urges me to extreme measures," says Angelique, "and with this knife I will kill myself here."

"Ah! ah! happy hour," replies Dandin.

But when Angelique says that he will surely be accused of killing her, he decides foolishly to go to her assistance and let her in the house.

But his wife slips past him in the darkness, closes the door, and turns the tables completely upon her husband. When her parents arrive she accuses Dandin of being drunk and of returning home late at night. Having this proof before them, M. de Sotenville and his wife again force the unhappy Dandin to demand pardon, this time on his knees.

The play closes with a final soliloquy in which Dandin says that with such a wife, the only thing for him to do is to jump headlong into the water.

Scene from The Miser.

THE MISER

THE MISER

(L'AVARE)

CHARACTERS IN THE PLAY

HARPAGON: father of Cleante and Elise.   In love with Mariane.

CLEANTE: Harpagon's son, and Mariane's suitor.

VALERE: son of Anselme, and Elise's suitor.

ANSELME: father of Valere and Mariane.

MASTER SIMON: agent.

MASTER JACQUES: cook and coachman to Harpagon.

LA FLECHE: Cleante's valet.

BRINDAVOINE: ⎫
                      ⎬ Harpagon's lackeys.
LA MERLUCHE: ⎭

A COMMISSIONER AND HIS CLERK.

ELISE: Harpagon's daughter and Valere's sweetheart.

MARIANE: Cleante's sweetheart; also beloved by Harpagon.

FROSINE: a designing woman.

MISTRESS CLAUDE: Harpagon's servant.

The scene is in Paris in Harpagon's House.

ACT I.

The play opens with Elise, the daughter of the miser Harpagon, pledging her love to Valere, who, in order to woo her, has assumed the duties of Harpagon's steward. At first, however, Elise hesitates to commit herself, because she fears that Valere may be like other men and transfer his affections to another.

She is also afraid to confess her love for Valere to her father, since his whole life is c e n t e r e d in his money. Cleante, her brother, confides his love for Mariane, a young woman who dwells in a neighboring house with her widowed mother.

The irascible nature of Harpagon is first shown in an altercation with La Fleche, his son's valet. After first searching him for stolen articles, Harpagon drives him out of the room. As soon as La Fleche has left, the miser thinks out loud about the 10,000 crowns that he has just buried in a casket in the garden, and of his fears for their safety.

When his son and daughter appear on the scene, Harpagon tells them that he wishes to speak to them about marriage. He describes Mariane and announces his intention of marrying her. He then fills them with consternation by stating that he has chosen Anselme, a friend and companion of his own age, as a husband for Elise.

Valere arrives and Harpagon asks his opinion of the choice that he has made for his daughter. "Anselme is a nobleman," says the miser, and then adds gleefully, "He has agreed to take Elise without a dowry."

Valere pretends to agree with H a r p a g o n, and then, while the miser has left to see if his gold is still safe, he takes the opportunity to urge Elise to pretend to yield to her father's wishes. "We'll find some pretext to break it off," says Valere confidently.

ACT II.

Cleante has been trying to borrow 15,000 francs and
has sent La Fleche to arrange terms with Master Simon,
who is an agent for the lender. La Fleche reports that 25
per cent is demanded and that part of the loan must consist of an assortment of old jewelry and furniture. Cleante
is beside himself with rage. While he is cursing the usur-
er, Simon appears and reveals, first to Cleante, that his
father is the lender, and then to Harpagon, that his son is
the borrower. Harpagon berates his son as a spendthrift
and a wastrel and drives him from the house.

Frosine, a woman who is very clever in the art of ca-
jolery and deceit, arrives on the scene and tries her hand
at securing money from Harpagon. She has been making
arrangements for his marriage with Mariane and now
asks for payment. Her efforts are to no avail.

ACT III.

Harpagon decides to give a dinner in honor of Mariane
and he also offers her the use of his coach so that she and
her mother can attend the fair. Master Jacques, his coachman and cook combined, suggests that his master give
him some money so that he can prepare a respectable
dinner. The suggestion does not appeal to the penurious
soul of Harpagon. Jacques also states that the horses are
so weak from lack of food that they can scarcely walk.

Valere gets into the good graces of the miser by means
of flattery and by quoting to him the words of "an ancient" philosopher: "It is necessary to eat in order to
live, but not to live in order to eat." Valere has a dis-
agreement with Jacques, who resolves to have his revenge on him.

Mariane arrives at the house and Harpagon introduces

her to his children. Cleante, p r e t e n d i n g to press his
father's suit, gives her a number of compliments, a fact
which very much disturbs the old man. He also removes
a large diamond ring from Harpagon's finger and presents
it to Mariane.

ACT IV.

Cleante urges M a r i a n e to win the consent of her
mother to their marriage. In this appeal he is aided by
Frosine, who says that she will assist the case as much as
possible. Harpagon, suspicious of his son's attitude toward
Mariane, determines to test him. Cleante tells his father
that there is no one whom he would rather have for his
mother-in-law, and this leads Harpagon to believe that he
himself would not care to marry her. Harpagon, in his
turn, tells his son that he really has planned to have Cleante marry Mariane instead of himself. Cleante falls into
this trap and declares his love for her. The two then have
hot words and are on the point of blows when Jacques arrives and effects a reconciliation. This he achieves by
making each believe that the other has given up his design
of marriage.

In the meantime La Fleche has discovered the casket
of money, buried in the garden, and he presents it to his
master. Harpagon soon discovers the theft and the scene
ends with his wild lamentations.

ACT V.

Harpagon hires a commissioner to help him discover
the thief. Jacques, desiring to have his r e v e n g e upon
Valere and hoping thus to get into the good graces of his
master, accuses Valere of the theft. He asserts that he
saw Valere carrying a "large-small" casket, "greyish-

red'' in color, which undoubtedly contained the stolen
money. Harpagon is willing to believe anything, and, when
Valere appears, he accuses him of the robbery. Valere
confesses that he has just stolen a treasure from Harpagon and asks for forgiveness. After a bitter discussion
Harpagon learns that Valere means that he has asked
Elise to marry him. This greatly increases the miser's
wrath.

Finally Anselme appears on the scene and Harpagon
relates his misfortunes to him. Harpagon speaks bitterly
of Valere, which leads the young man to confess that he is
the son of a certain famous noble of Naples, who has been
believed lost at sea some sixteen years earlier with his
wife and two children. Mariane, who is present, declares
that she is the daughter of this same nobleman, she and
her mother having escaped alive from the wreck. Anselme,
in his turn, admits that he is the nobleman himself and is
thus the father of Valere and Mariane.

While these astonishing revelations appear to solve
all the problems, they do not appease Harpagon, who is
still searching for his money. Cleante then tells his father
that he knows where the money is hidden and will return
it, provided Harpagon relinquishes all claim to Mariane.
This the miser agrees to do. But before being completely
reconciled, he makes Anselme pay the fees of the commissioner whom he had employed to help him recover his
money.

MONSIEUR DE POURCEAUGNAC

MONSIEUR DE POURCEAUGNAC

CHARACTERS IN THE PLAY

M. DE POURCEAUGNAC: a wealthy man from Limousin.

ORONTE: father of Julie.

JULIE: daughter of Oronte.

NERINE: a lady of intrigue, Julie's maid.

LUCETTE: a woman pretending to be from Gascony.

ERASTE: lover of Julie.

SBRIGANI: a Neapolitan; a man of intrigue.

FIRST PHYSICIAN

SECOND PHYSICIAN

AN APOTHECARY

A MALE PEASANT

A FEMALE PEASANT

FIRST AND SECOND MUSICIANS

FIRST AND SECOND LAWYERS

FIRST SWISS

SECOND SWISS

A POLICE OFFICER

TWO ARCHERS

Several Musicians, Players of Instruments, and Dancers.

The Scene is in Paris.

ACT I.

Eraste comes to serenade and meet his beloved Julie, which must be done by stealth since her father, Oronte, has forbidden the two lovers to see one another. He has chosen for his daughter's husband a certain Monsieur de Pourceaugnac, a wealthy Limousine.

The suit of Eraste is aided by Sbrigani, a Neapolitan given to intrigue, and by Nerine, Julie's confidante, who is also trained in cunning. Julie is very much afraid that she will be forced to marry Pourceaugnac, but Eraste calms her fears. He advises her not to oppose the will of her father, telling her that a plan has been devised by means of which it will be possible to get rid of the obnoxious lover.

When the rival appears on the scene he is made sport of by the people on the street. As presented on the stage, in the person of Moliere himself, Pourceaugnac was garishly dressed in a costume described as "howling in colors." As he berates the people for their ridicule, and threatens to engage in fisticuffs with the first one who laughs, he is rescued from his troubles by Sbrigani.

Eraste then appears and pretends that he recognizes Pourceaugnac as an old friend. Although he gets mixed up in his identifications of the relatives whom he says he knows, mistaking an aunt for an uncle, for example, finally, with the assistance of Sbrigani, he persuades Pourceaugnac to come to his house as a guest.

While the stranger is at Eraste's home, the latter hires two physicians to come and examine his guest for some pretended ailment. Although Pourceaugnac protests that he is not ill, the physicians assure him that they know better than he does how his health is. "It is a bad sign," says one of them, "when an invalid does not know when he is ill."

Moliere, by means of a lengthy dialogue between the physicians on the symptoms of their victim, again reveals his antipathy toward the medical profession of his day. The outcome of this diagnosis is the conclusion that Pourceaugnac is suffering from melancholy and hypochondria. Pourceaugnac is wholly at a loss to explain the action of the two physicians.

"For an hour," he says, "I have listened to your comedy. What do you wish to impart to me by your gibberish and your nonsense?"

He finally finds refuge from their importunities by flight. "What the deuce," says he as he departs. "Are all the people in this country crazy? I have never seen the like before, and I don't understand it."

ACT II.

As soon as Pourceaugnac has fled, Sbrigani tells one of the physicians to go to the house of Oronte and inform him that his prospective son-in-law is afflicted with a terrible disease. This the physician proceeds to do and when Oronte demands to know the nature of the illness the charlatan says that it is not ethical for him to reveal it.

Sbrigani then renews his attack in another direction. Dressing himself as a Flemish merchant, he goes to Oronte's house and tries to collect some bills which he claims that M. Pourceaugnac owes him. Having thus put Oronte in a proper frame of mind toward the fiscal responsibilities of his prospective son-in-law, Sbrigani turns his attention to Pourceaugnac himself.

After pretending sympathy with the much-hectored man, especially with respect to his bout with the physicians, he inquires into his affair with Julie. Under protestations of friendship, the wily rogue insinuates that he knows some secret respecting his prospective wife that Pourceaugnac should hear about, but that his conscience will not let him reveal it. Finally, under pressure, he says: "To tell you that this young lady leads a dishonest life is too much, and to apply to her the word *galante* is not enough; but to say that she is a coquette is about right."

Because of these machinations of the Neapolitan, the meeting between Oronte and Pourceaugnac is considerably strained. Julie is apparently anxious to meet the stranger, but her father will not permit the introduction, nor is he on his part eager for it.

"When is it that you wish me to marry Monsieur?" asks Julie naively.

"Never," replies Oronte; "he is not for you."

While this matter is being debated Lucette and Nerine appear and both claim Pourceaugnac as their husband. They say that he had married them several years before and now has deserted them. During the ensuing uproar three children appear and beset the beleaguered Limousine with cries that he is their father.

"To the devil with these guttersnipes," shouts the poor man.

The bewildered Pourceaugnac is at his wits end when Sbrigani appears and offers his help. He urges the stranger to get legal advice and offers to take him to some attorneys whom he knows. "But they have a peculiar habit," warns the Neapolitan, "since they sing at their work."

To this Pourceaugnac replies that he cares not how they talk, if only they will tell him what he wants to know. But since his conversation with them is carried on in verse, the poor stranger is driven to distraction and all that he learns is that bigamy is a hanging matter.

ACT III.

Because of the capital nature of the crime of which Pourceaugnac has been accused, Sbrigani says that his only hope to escape his fate is to flee to his own country. Although the stranger shouts for justice, since he is innocent, he finally agrees to the Neapolitan's scheme and allows himself to be dressed in women's clothes.

After Sbrigani has left "to find a better hood," Pourceaugnac is insulted by two Swiss guards who are searching for him, and when he is rescued from their importunities his identity is discovered. Although all seems lost, the wily Neapolitan bribes the police officer to permit the escape of Pourceaugnac, and this the latter does without further loss of time.

Immediately after the flight of the victimized Limousine, Eraste arrives on the scene with Julie, whom he declares that he has just rescued from the clutches of the stranger, while the latter was attempting to abduct her.

This bravery of Eraste so pleases Oronte that he gives his consent to the marriage of his daughter with her lover. "And I am so delighted," said Oronte, "that I will endow the marriage of my daughter with some ten thousand crowns. Send for the notary to prepare the contract."

"And while we are waiting for him," replies the happy Eraste, "let us divert ourselves by witnessing some masques which the news of the impending marriage of Monsieur de Pourceaugnac has attracted from all parts of the city."

THE MAGNIFICENT LOVERS

THE MAGNIFICENT LOVERS
(LES AMANTS MAGNIFIQUES)

CHARACTERS IN THE PLAY

ARISTIONE: Princess, mother of Eriphile.

ERIPHILE: daughter of the Princess.

CLEONICE: confidante of Eriphile.

CHOREBE: member of the retinue of the Princess.

IPHICRATE, TIMOCLES: the magnificent lovers.

SOSTRATE: general of the army and lover of Eriphile.

CLITIDAS: court jester in the retinue of Eriphile.

ANAXARQUE: an astrologer.

CLEON: son of Anaxarque.

A FALSE VENUS: in league with Anaxarque.

The Scene is laid in Thessaly in the delightful Vale of Tempe.

The play of the *Magnificent Lovers* opens with an introduction in which the French King, representing Neptune,
appears with a number of his nobles. The elaborate nature
of the stage setting may be appreciated by the following
description provided by Moliere:

"The theater opens to the agreeable sound of many
instruments and reveals to the eyes a vast sea, girt on
each side by four great rocks. The summits of these each
carry a River marked with symbols after the manner of
deities. At the base of the rocks there are a dozen Tritons-
on each side, and in the middle of the sea four Cupids
are mounted on dolphins. Aeolus commands the winds to
die down, and while the Cupids, the Tritons, and the Rivers
reply to him, the sea calms, and in the midst of the waves
an island appears.

"Eight fishermen emerge from the sea bringing pieces
of mother-of-pearl and branches of coral, who after a
merry dance, seat themselves upon a rock beneath the
Rivers. A chorus of musicians then announce the coming
of Neptune, and while this god dances with his followers,
the fishermen, the Tritons, and the Rivers accompany
his steps in d i f f e r e n t m a n n e r s to the sound of pearl
conches. The entire spectacle is a magnificent *galanterie*
in which one of the royal princes directs upon the sea the
promenade of the princesses."

ACT I.

The first act introduces Sostrate, a famous general
of the army, and Clitidas, the court jester, who, however,
is a man of considerable observation and sense. Clitidas
tells Sostrate that he has discovered the latter's secret
love for Eriphile, who is the daughter of Princess Aristione, the ruler of the realm. The jester says that he desires to aid the general in this affair. Sostrate is very

much afraid that Eriphile will discover his love and think him presumptuous, so he swears the jester to silence.

The two rival princes, Iphicrate and Timocles, (the magnificent lovers of the play), are suing for the hand of Eriphile, and have provided a lavish celebration in honor of her and her mother. They have just witnessed a display given by Iphicrate, who for the moment is the favorite. Sostrate, on account of his love for Eriphile, did not attend the celebration.

The princes report that they have not had much success in their suit for the hand of Eriphile, the cause of which Aristione believes is to be found in her daughter's indecision. She then asks Sostrate to visit the princess and discover which of the two suitors she prefers for her husband. Clitidas promises to help each prince in his suit for Eriphile, although he really favors Sostrate. The princess, herself, is represented as being unhappy amd melancholy in spite of the various celebrations given to divert her.

ACT II.

Clitidas comes to visit the princess and to ascertain how she feels toward Sostrate. When he tells Eriphile that the general is in love and infers that it is with the princess, she is very indignant at his audacity. Then the jester replies that it is not actually the princess with whom he is in love, but with a young lady, Arsinoe by name, who is one of her maids. This greatly surprises Eriphile and she forces Clitidas to tell her the truth.

Sostrate arrives to carry out the order of Aristione and to discover which of the princes is the favored one. Eriphile refuses to tell, but instead asks Sostrate which one he would prefer. While they are discussing this point, the princess is summoned to witness a play in the forest of Diana.

This elaborate interlude is a pastoral, which has for its theme the unrequited love of a shepherd for a shepherdess and the eventual victory for the constancy of the lover. The interlude concludes with a quarrel between the two lovers and their final reconciliation.

ACT III.

Eriphile tells her mother that she is unable to make a decision between Iphicrate and Timocles on account of her irresolution. Her real reason, however, is that she is in love with Sostrate.

Anaxarque, an astrologer, says that he will discover by means of his art and the position of the stars, which prince would make the better husband. Although some doubts are expressed as to the power of Anaxarque to discover this, it is finally agreed to let him try his skill, especially since Aristione believes in him.

The party then departs to witness another spectacle in a neighboring grotto, where eight Statues, carrying torches, execute a series of dances.

ACT IV.

This act opens with a dialogue between Eriphile and her mother on the matter of her choice of a suitor. Aristione urges her daughter to reveal her heart to her and the name of the person who has won her affection. When Eriphile refuses to do this, the goddess Venus appears and states that she herself will reveal the name of the one who would make the best husband for the princess.

In the meantime Anaxarque, with the aid of his son Cleon, has prepared an artifice by means of which he intends to impose upon the superstition of Aristione. Since, between the two princes, Iphicrate has made Anaxarque

the best offer to select this prince as the successful suit-
or, he will be designated by the astrologer. Anaxarque, in
his delight, assures his son that "our fortune is made."

Eriphile encounters Sostrate and without more ado
presents him with the direct question: "Sostrate, do you
love me?" When the general answers this question eva-
sively, Eriphile replies for him and declares her own
love. Sostrate is unwilling to believe his good fortune and
in his confusion he merely asks that when the princess is
married she will deign some time to think of him. Eriphile
then sends him away half in anger and half in sorrow.
Cleonice, her confidante, tries to cheer the princess and
asks that she witness some dancers who have arrived.
"Yes, Cleonice," she says, "let them do what they wish,
provided only that they leave me to my thoughts."

ACT V.

Clitidas arrives bringing the news that heaven has just
declared who should be the husband of the princess. Eriphile sharply bids the jester to leave her, since she believes that fate has decreed for her one of the two princes.
Thereupon Clitidas announces that if she does not want to
hear the news about Sostrate, he will withdraw. This threat
brings Eriphile to her senses and she asks eagerly for
his message.

The jester then states that the general has just saved
her mother from death by slaying a wild boar that had
attacked the royal party, and that the two princes in the
face of danger had behaved in a cowardly fashion. In recognition of his bravery Aristione had promised her daughter to Sostrate.

Iphicrate and Timocles are very angry at the princess
for deciding against them and declare that they will always
be enemies of her realm. Despite these threats, the party

goes to see the celebration of the Feast of the Parthian Games. And thus, to the tunes of lively music and the spectacle of merry dancers, the play ends happily for all concerned except the magnificent lovers.

LE MISANTROPE

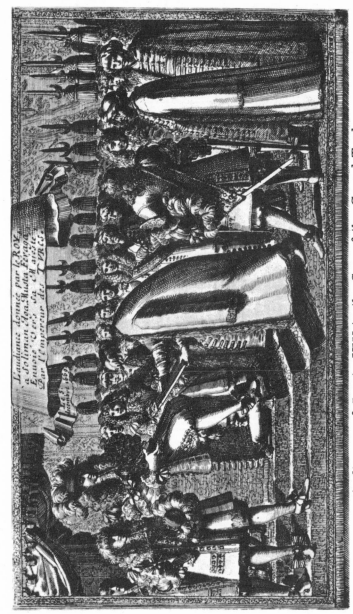

Audience of Louis XIV to the Son of the Grand Turk.
(The Bourgeois Gentleman).

THE BOURGEOIS GENTLEMAN

THE BOURGEOIS GENTLEMAN

(LE BOURGEOIS GENTILHOMME)

CHARACTERS IN THE PLAY

MONSIEUR JOURDAIN: the bourgeois.

MADAME JOURDAIN: his wife.

LUCILE: the daughter of M. Jourdain.

NICOLE: a servant.

CLEONTE: Lucile's lover.

COVIELLE: valet of Cleonte.

DORANTE: count, lover of Dorimene.

DORIMENE: marquise.

MUSIC MASTER

PUPIL OF THE MUSIC MASTER

DANCING MASTER

FENCING MASTER

MASTER OF PHILOSOPHY

MASTER TAILOR

ASSISTANT TO THE TAILOR

TWO LACKEYS

Several Musicians, Instrument Players, Dancers, Cooks, Journeymen Tailors, and Other Persons in the Ballet.

The Scene is in Paris.

ACT I.

This play is characterized as a "comedy ballet," since it is interspersed with interludes of dancing and music, which add a lively atmosphere to the normal stage action. It opens with an overture in the home of M. Jourdain, a foolish man of the middle class, a bourgeois, who has determined to become a nobleman. This he is attempting to accomplish by a lavish expenditure of money.

Following the overture a Music Master and a Dancing Master discuss the situation and congratulate one another over the fine opportunity which M. Jourdain's generosity affords them to fill their purses. They both wish, however, that he himself had a deeper understanding of their arts.

M. Jourdain arrives to receive his music and dancing lessons. He appears wearing a dressing gown and a night-cap, but, as he immediately reveals, the gown conceals tight-fitting knee breeches and a jacket, one of red and the other of green velvet. This costume, he fondly believes, represents the height of fashion.

The musicians then sing a song which M. Jourdain characterizes as lugubrious. "You should put a little more merriment here and there into it," he says. To this the Music Master replies that the music must be suitable to the words.

"Let me show you," says M. Jourdain. "I learned a pretty little song in my youth. It has a sheep in it." "A sheep?" exclaims the Dancing Master incredulously. Whereupon M. Jourdain sings a ludicrous ditty in which the heroine is described as being "as sweet as a sheep," but "as cruel as a tiger." The two masters are forced to agree that it is, indeed, a pretty song. They then praise their respective arts and their students present exhibitions before M. Jourdain.

ACT II.

In this act, which is a continuation of the first, the Music Master and the Dancing Master proceed to give M. Jourdain lessons in their respective arts. In this instruction, however, he shows himself to be quite without the necessary ability to profit by it. A Fencing Master now arrives to instruct the bourgeois in the use of the sword. But of the simplest rudiments of this art the latter again shows himself to be completely ignorant.

An argument soon develops between the three teachers with respect to the virtues of their respective subjects, each praising his own and disparaging the others. The three masters finally come to blows in spite of the best efforts of M. Jourdain to quiet them. At this crucial moment a Master of Philosophy appears upon the scene and the quarreling teachers decide to let him settle their dispute. The philosopher accepts the task, which he executes merely by praising his own profession. This leads finally to a pitched battle between all four of the masters. They depart vituperating each other, while M. Jourdain sorrowfully says: "Let them fight as much as they please. I wouldn't soil my robe to separate them. And besides, if I tried, I might myself receive some of their blows."

The philosopher returns, mending his robe, to give M. Jourdain his lesson, which had been interrupted by the fight. He introduces the bourgeois into the mysteries of phonetics to the latter's great delight. He also teaches him the difference between prose and poetry, a matter which surprises M. Jourdain very much.

When the lesson has been concluded, a Master Tailor and his assistant appear bringing with them a suit of many colors, which M. Jourdain has ordered. The latter wishes this to be fitted to him in the latest style, whereupon a group of apprentices appear, who adorn him in the new raiment. In the course of this process they engage in a lively dance appropriate to the occasion.

ACT III.

M. Jourdain summons his servants in order to issue instructions about a dinner which he is planning to give. He is clad in his new clothes, which he is eager to exhibit to the citizens of the city. He is much disconcerted, however, when his servant Nicole bursts into loud laughter at seeing him in his gay raiment. And his anger increases as she seems unable to control her mirth.

Madame Jourdain appears upon the scene and expresses in unmistakable language her opinion of her husband's actions. "You are the laughing stock of the world," she says. M. Jourdain, however, tries to make her understand his point of view by telling her some of the interesting things which he has just learned. But his wife, still unconvinced, maintains a dim view of the proceedings and is aided by appropriate comments from Nicole.

"The idea of taking dancing lessons at your age!" says Madame Jourdain. "Are you planning to kill someone?" asks Nicole, referring to his lessons in fencing. "Will you both hold your tongues," shouts the disconcerted M. Jourdain. He then explains what he has learned about orthography from the philosopher, to which his wife replies: "Bosh!"

At this juncture Dorante, an impecunious noble, who has been borrowing sums of money from M. Jourdain, arrives. The object of his visit is to increase his debt, which he hopes to achieve by the route of flattery. "I was speaking of you this morning in the chamber of the king," says the wily noble. Madame Jourdain, who sees through the count's scheme, expresses her view without restraint. "This man is making a milk cow of you," she says to her

husband. In spite of her objections, however, the foolish
bourgeois approves another loan for the count. "You are
a true dupe," says his wife.

M. Jourdain is secretly enamored of a marquise named
Dorimene, who lives close by, and he has been using
Dorante to bring about a better acquaintance between them.
To further this enterprise he proposes to give a dinner
that evening in his house after he has sent Madame Jourdain away to pay a visit to her sister. Through Nicole,
however, she learns about the plan and proposes to frus-
trate it.

Cleonte, a young man of respectable, but not noble
birth, is in love with Lucile, the daughter of the Jourdains.
Unfortunately he has been led to believe that she has played
him false and he has come with Covielle, his valet, to say
farewell to her. Covielle, who is in love with Nicole, has
a similar suspicion of his beloved. The two young men encounter Lucile and Nicole and a lively altercation ensues,
in which the suitors heap recriminations upon the ladies,
but will not allow them to make any explanation about their
conduct. Finally, however, the truth comes out. Lucile
attributes their behavior to the lectures of an old aunt
whose firm belief it is that all men are devils and should
be sedulously avoided. The folly of this advice is admitted
and the lovers are reunited.

Madame Jourdain, who favors the match between Cleonte and Lucile, urges the young man to ask M. Jourdain
for his consent to the marriage. But when he follows this
advice, he is forced to admit that he is not of noble birth
and negotiations are immediately broken off by the ambi-
tious bourgeois.

After these matters have been concluded, Dorante and
Dorimene arrive at the home of M. Jourdain. The marquise, however, is reluctant to dine at a house where she
knows no one, but Dorante persuades her that the dinner

is actually being given at an inn and that M. Jourdain is its host. The bourgeois has entrusted Dorante with a diamond to be presented to the marquise in his name, but the crafty count, who is himself in love with Dorimene, has given it to her as coming from himself. The act ends as the party is preparing for the dinner, which is being prepared by a group of waiters who dance together in a ballet as they work.

ACT IV.

While the party is at dinner and things are going merrily with song and dance appropriate to the lavish food, Madame Jourdain arrives upon the scene. She expresses herself in no uncertain terms about the perfidy of a husband, who would give such an elaborate dinner, while he sends his wife away to visit her sister. Her lamentations and sharp comments soon break up the party. Dorante and Dorimene hastily depart to the dismay of their host.

While M. Jourdain is lamenting this unfortunate state of affairs, Covielle arrives in disguise and tells him that the son of the Grand Turk himself wishes to marry Lucile. M. Jourdain is greatly flattered at this proposed alliance. Covielle tells the gullible man that the young Turk, who is really Cleonte in disguise, has heard of the beautiful daughter of Monsieur Jourdain, a noble of Paris. He continues with the statement that the young man, in order to have a father-in-law of sufficient dignity, proposes to make M. Jourdain a mamamouchi. This title, he explains, is a very grand one in his country, and is equivalent to the title of paladin in France.

The ceremony, necessary in bestowing this honor, is immediately carried out in a very impressive and elaborate manner. This scene is really the highlight of the comedy, and much of the unusual success of the play has been attributed to the ballet of the Turkish ceremony with which the act ends.

ACT V.

M. Jourdain breaks the splendid news to his wife that he has been made a mamamouchi, but she does not appear to be very much impressed by this information. As he attempts to explain the meaning of the honor that has been bestowed upon him, she decides that he has finally lost his mind.

At this time Dorante and Dorimene arrive. They have just decided to get married as soon as possible. Since this decision is unknown to M. Jourdain, he attempts to discover the effect upon the marquise of his gift of the diamond, but about this matter the count is understandably evasive.

Lucile is then informed by her father that she is to become the wife of the son of the Grand Turk. To this she makes violent objection until she recognizes Cleonte in his disguise. Madame Jourdain also voices strenuous disapproval of the match, but Covielle is finally able to explain the situation to her. Whereupon she also gives her consent.

M. Jourdain then sends for a notary, and as they await his arrival, Dorante and Dorimene announce that this would be an appropriate time also for their own marriage. This unexpected news M. Jourdain hears with consternation, although at first he believes that it must be a joke. Nicole then says that she also would like to be married to Covielle, to which M. Jourdain agrees.

Thus the play ends happily for all concerned except for the poor bourgeois, who concludes the ceremony by offering his wife to whoever wants her.

PSYCHE

PSYCHE

CHARACTERS IN THE PLAY

JUPITER

VENUS

CUPID

AEGIALE, PHAENE: Graces.

PSYCHE

THE KING: father of Psyche.

AGLAURE: sister of Psyche.

CIDIPPE: sister of Psyche.

CLEOMENE, AGENOR: princes and lovers of Psyche.

ZEPHYR

LYCAS

THE RIVER GOD

The Scenes are Elaborate Stage Settings Appropriate to the Varying Aspects of the Opera.

The opera *Psyche,* the longest of the works of Moliere, was a collaboration with Pierre Corneille (1606-1684), the greatest of the French tragic poets. The words of the choruses were written by Philippe Quinault (1635-1688), a celebrated composer of plays and librettos, and the musical scores by Jean Baptiste Lully (Lulli) (1632-1687), called the founder of the National French Opera. To augment this galaxy of artists, spectacular stage settings were provided, which were implemented by special machines designed to effect the scenes. The play was first presented before the King in January, 1671 and opened to the public in July of that same year.

The opera is an extravaganza based upon the classical myth of Cupid and Psyche. It opens with a long prologue in addition to which elaborate interludes are provided between the acts.

The opening scene presents in the foreground a rural place and in the backround a rock pierced by an opening through which a prospect of the sea is visible.

ACT I.

The first act of the play begins with a conversation between Aglaure and Cidippe, the two sisters of Psyche. The young ladies are jealous since Psyche is receiving a great deal of attention because of her beauty and has in the train of her followers the two princes Cleomene and Agenor. With these young men the two sisters are in love.

Although Cleomene and Agenor are both rivals for the hand of Psyche, they are also close friends, and they decide to leave the choice between them to Psyche herself. But this Psyche refuses to make and advises them to turn their attentions to her two sisters.

At this moment Lycas, a captain of the guard, arrives with an urgent message from Psyche's father, the King.

The fearful news contained in this communication states that the oracle has demanded that Psyche be abandoned in a desert place, where she will be seized by a monster, described as "a serpent who spreads his venom everywhere and in his rage troubles both the earth and sky." This sad fate destined for their sister does not seem to overwhelm Aglaure and Cidippe with grief.

The scene of the interlude between Acts I and II reveals a desert filled with horrendous rocks and one sees in the distance what is described as a terrifying grotto. A troop of people appear who deplore the sad fate of Psyche with plaintive songs and words of despair.

ACT II.

The second act opens with a conversation between Psyche and her father, the King. The King is unwilling that his daughter should be left for the monster to devour, and yet he fears to disobey the mandate of the oracle.

Psyche is unafraid and demands that she be left in the deserted spot, a resolution that pleases her sisters, who then will no longer have a rival. Cleomene and Agenor arrive and offer their services to Psyche, saying that they will slay the monster and free her from her peril.

While Psyche is trying to dissuade them from their purpose, two Zephyrs bear her off through the air, while Cupid, flying above, condemns his two rivals to death for having dared to strive with a god.

The scene of the second interlude between Acts II and III reveals a magnificent court. It is decorated with stone columns enriched with golden figures, and forms a grand palace which Cupid has designed for Psyche. Six Cyclops attended by six fairies carrying large silver vases, dance a ballet, which is accompanied by a recitative by the god Vulcan.

ACT III.

This act reveals Psyche enjoying the marvels of the splendid palace and rich gardens which Cupid has constructed for her after her rescue from the desert and the dragon.

While she is wondering what is to become of her, Cupid reveals himself as a young man and gives her the pleasing information that he is the monster described by the oracle. Cupid makes love to her, but will not reveal his identity.

Psyche says that she has left her father and her two sisters believing that she has perished and that she desires to inform them of her safety and good fortune.

In the third interlude between Acts III and IV, there is no change of scene, but a ballet is danced by four Cupids and four Zephyrs, accompanied by a dialogue chanted between one of the Cupids and one of the Zephyrs.

ACT IV.

Acceding to the wishes of Psyche, Cupid has her two sisters brought to the palace, where they are informed of the good fortune that has befallen their sister. But this revelation only increases their jealousy and they are returned to earth.

Psyche continues to ask Cupid to reveal his identity and finally, yielding to her importunities, he tells her his true name. Immediately upon this fact being known, the scene changes. The magnificent palace disappears and Psyche finds herself alone upon a vast field. Along its edge flows a great river into which she wishes to throw herself. While she is bewailing her lot she sees the river god seated upon a heap of rushes and reeds and leaning against a great urn from which gushes a flow of water.

The river god comforts her, revealing that her troubles stem from the anger and jealousy which have been aroused in Venus by Cupid's love for her. Perhaps these will abate after a while, says the river god.

But it soon becomes evident that this reconciliation is not imminent, for Venus herself appears and upbraids Psyche for daring to love a god. Although Psyche protests that it is the god who has fallen in love with her, Venus will not listen and casts the poor young lady into Hades.

In the fourth interlude between Acts IV and V, the scene represents the infernal regions. One beholds there a fiery sea, the waves of which are in violent agitation. This frightful sea is rimmed with burning ruins and in the midst of the waves, and across what is called a hideous mouth, appears the infernal palace of Pluto. Eight furies appear and dance a ballet, rejoicing in the rage awakened in the soul of the sweetest of the divinities (Venus). A hob-goblin mixes his acrobatics with the dances, while Psyche passes by in Charon's boat with a box which she has received from Proserpina for Venus.

ACT V.

While Psyche is deploring her hard fate, she suddenly meets the two princes, Cleomene and Agenor, who inform her that they have been cast into Hades for having loved her and thus having aroused the anger of Cupid. They are finally compelled to depart and Psyche laments the fact that they should endure this sad misfortune on account of their constancy and love for her.

Cupid, who has not forgotten Psyche, comes to find her and is met by his mother, Venus. A stormy scene immediately follows between mother and son and they finally decide to carry the matter before Jupiter for arbitration.

Scene from Psyche.

At this point there are lightning and rolls of thunder and Jupiter appears in the air supported by an eagle. After the king of the gods has heard both sides of the question, he decides in favor of Cupid, and the two lovers are united.

In an elaborate epilogue two great machines descend to the stage, one on each side of Jupiter. Venus and her suite mount into one and Cupid with Psyche into the other and all ascend into Heaven. The play ends with a great chorus of songs and a sprightly mixture of dances as the gods celebrate the fete attending the wedding of Cupid and Psyche.

THE ROGUERIES OF SCAPIN

THE ROGUERIES OF SCAPIN

(LES FOURBERIES DE SCAPIN)

CHARACTERS IN THE PLAY

ARGANTE: father of Octave and Zerbinette.

GERONTE: father of Leandre and Hyacinte.

OCTAVE: son of Argante and lover of Hyacinte.

LEANDRE: son of Geronte and lover of Zerbinette.

ZERBINETTE: believed to be an Egyptian girl, but discovered to be the daughter of Argante; beloved by Leandre.

HYACINTE: daughter of Geronte and beloved by Octave.

SCAPIN: valet of Leandre and a knave.

SILVESTRE: valet of Octave.

NERINE: nurse of Hyacinte.

CARLE: a knave.

TWO PORTERS

The Scene is in Naples.

ACT I.

While Argante, the father of Octave, and Geronte, the father of Leandre, were away on a business trip they left their sons in the care of the respective valets of the young men. Silvestre is the valet of Octave and Scapin the valet of Leandre.

Scapin is characterized as a knave. He himself admits the charge and describes his attainments in these words: "There is no doubt that I have received from Heaven a genius well adapted to the fabrication of those pretty tricks of the spirit, of the ingenious intrigues to which the common ignoramuses give the name of rogueries; and I am able to say without vanity that one has scarcely ever seen a man who is more skillful in designing schemes and intrigues, or who has acquired more glory in this noble craft."

While his father has been away, Octave has fallen in love with Hyacinte, a beautiful young lady whom he had met quite by chance and of whose antecedents he was in ignorance. So violent was his attachment that Nerine, the nurse who had the custody of Hyacinte, would not encourage his suit unless he married her ward.

At this juncture Silvestre informs Octave that his father has unexpectedly returned and that he wishes his son to marry a daughter of Geronte, who is being sent by an uncle from Taranto for this purpose. In this dilemma Octave appeals to Scapin for aid, and this the rogue promises to give him. Scapin advises him to be firm with his father, but when Octave sees Argante approaching he flees in dismay.

Argante has learned of his son's love for Hyacinte and arrives on the scene in a very angry mood. Scapin at first sympathizes with him and then urges that he take no steps in the matter to oppose the marriage of his son; but in this the father remains obdurate. In the course of the conversation Scapin hints that Leandre has behaved even worse than Octave.

ACT II.

When Geronte and Argante meet each other, the former begins to sympathize with the latter on account of the behavior of his son. This annoys Argante, who then reveals to his friend what Scapin had told him relative to the conduct of Leandre. This worries Geronte very much and he immediately accosts Leandre and asks him to explain what he has done, stating that Scapin is his authority in the matter.

This in turn arouses the anger of Leandre and when he meets his valet he is barely restrained from running him through with his sword. Upon pressure Scapin confesses to a number of tricks which he has played upon Leandre, but denies that he has told anything to Geronte. The evil act that Leandre has committed is merely that of loving a beautiful Egyptian girl named Zerbinette.

This conversation is terminated when Carle, a cheat, arrives with the news that the Egyptians are about to leave with Zerbinette unless they are paid a substantial sum of money. In his distress Leandre turns to Scapin for help, but the latter now berates him for his unjust accusation. However, he is finally persuaded, not only by Leandre, but also by his friend Octave, to undertake the mission and raise the necessary money.

"I shall obtain it from your fathers," says the wily scamp.

Scapin first meets Argante and tells him that for a large sum of money he will be able to break the attachment between his son and Hyacinte.

"How much?" demands Argante.

"Two hundred pistoles," replies Scapin.

"Away with you! We will go to law," shouts Argante.

But at this critical moment in the negotiations, Silvestre, dressed as a fighter, arrives on the stage, and representing himself as the brother of Hyacinte, so frightens Argante that he gives Scapin the money.

Thus successful with Argante, Scapin next turns his attention to Geronte, whom he greatly distresses by telling him that Leandre has been kidnapped by Turks, and that they demand a heavy ransom.

"Five hundred crowns they ask," says the scamp.

"The devil take us! Five hundred crowns?" screams Geronte.

"We must hurry," replies Scapin. "They carry him away with them in their galley in two hours."

After some further parley, Geronte finally suggests that Scapin, out of his affection for and his loyalty to his master, should give himself up to the Turks in place of Leandre. But Scapin readily points out that the abductors would certainly not exchange a person of his status for such a man as his master. Whereupon Geronte sees that he is beaten and is finally persuaded to part with his money.

ACT III.

Scapin and Silvestre accompany Zerbinette and Hyacinte to meet their lovers and assure them that everything will turn out well in the end.

Scapin meets Geronte and determines to have his revenge for some of the insults that he has received from him. He informs Geronte that a band of soldiers and relatives of Hyacinte, led by her irate brother, are out searching for him, since he is the one that has caused the marriage of Octave with Hyacinte to be broken off. He advises Geronte to seek safety by crawling into a sack. When the latter does this, Scapin holds conversations with imaginary individuals and at regular intervals beats Geronte in the sack.

Finally, however, Geronte detects the trick and Scapin is forced to seek safety in flight. While Geronte is swearing to have vengeance, Zerbinette arrives on the scene, and not recognizing Geronte as Leandre's father, tells him of the trick that Scapin has used to get the money from him. Geronte, breathing fire, denounces everyone and vows that he will send Scapin to the gibbet that very day.

When affairs are in this critical condition, the truth is finally revealed. It is discovered that Hyacinte is the daughter of Geronte and that Zerbinette is really the daughter of Argante, who was stolen at the age of four years by the Egyptians. Her identity is revealed by a bracelet, which she still possesses. And thus the clouds roll away and the plot unravels to the satisfaction of everyone except poor Scapin, whom Geronte still wishes to hang.

At this important moment Carle arrives with the news that the unfortunate Scapin, while passing a building, has been critically injured when the hammer of a stonecutter fell upon his head. He is brought upon the stage by two men, with his head swathed in bandages, a sight that arouses the pity of those assembled, with the exception of Geronte. When forgiveness is asked for him, this is acceded to by all except Geronte, who, however, says that he will join in the general amnesty provided Scapin dies. Thereupon the happy and reconciled group leave for a celebration dinner and Scapin says: "As for me, carry me to the end of the table, so that they may watch me die."

This, however, is Scapin's final jest, for when the play is presented the rascal rises to his feet and removes his bandages. His reported injury has been a hoax.

THE COUNTESS OF ESCARBAGNAS

THE COUNTESS OF ESCARBAGNAS

(LA COMTESSE D'ESCARBAGNAS)

CHARACTERS IN THE PLAY

THE COUNTESS OF ESCARBAGNAS

THE COUNT: her son.

THE VISCOUNT: lover of Julie.

JULIE: beloved by the Viscount.

MONSIEUR TIBAUDIER: a counselor, lover of the Countess.

MONSIEUR HARPIN: a tax collector, another lover of the Countess.

MONSIEUR BOBINET: tutor of the Count.

ANDREE: servant of the Countess.

JEANNOT: lackey of Monsieur Tibaudier.

CRIQUET: lackey of the Countess.

The Scene is in Angouleme.

This light comedy in one act concerns the romance between two young people whose love is thwarted by a quarrel between their families. The play opens with a conversation between the Viscount Cleante and Julie in which the latter chides her lover for being late to their meeting. They are compelled to conceal their love from others because of the family feud and this leads to various difficulties.

The Countess D'Escarbagnas, for example, thinks that the Viscount is in love with her instead of Julie, since he must pretend indifference to the latter. The Countess has just returned from Paris, where she had learned many of the customs in vogue at the court. Some of these she tries to enforce at home to the great disgust of the servants whom she is constantly scolding.

Julie, in an attempt to divert the attention of the Countess from the Viscount, suggests that a more suitable match for her in her high social position would be M. Harpin, a collector of taxes, or M. Tibaudier, a counselor.

The Viscount has prepared a comedy which is to be given in honor of the Countess and while they are getting ready to see it, Jeannot, the lackey of M. Tibaudier appears with a basket of pears and a letter. In this epistle the counselor states that the pears are not quite ripe, but that their condition is quite in keeping with the hardness of the Countess's heart toward him.

Close upon the receipt of the fruit the man himself arrives bearing with him a poem which he has written to express his love for the Countess. Although the verses have not been inspired by the highest muse, both Julie and the Viscount praise them.

"The epigrams are worthy of Martial!" exclaims the Viscount. "Martial?" asks the Countess. "I thought he made gloves."

But she appears pleased and does not disdain the limping verses.

As the guests are preparing to seat themselves to hear the comedy which the Viscount has prepared for them, the young son of the Countess appears with Bobinet, his tutor, and exhibits his learning by reciting in Latin the remarkable line that "all names which apply only to men should be masculine." The Countess is properly impressed with his progress.

As the guests are seating themselves, M. Harpin arrives and is informed that he is about to hear a play. However, he immediately declares his love for the Countess; but when he sees that she appears to be quite fond of both the Viscount and M. Tibaudier, he becomes very angry and exchanges bitter words with them. He especially accuses the Countess of favoring the suit of the Viscount, and thereupon he leaves in a rage.

Before the comedy can proceed, a message arrives for the Viscount, which he reads to the guests. It contains some very welcome news. "The quarrel between your parents and those of Julie has been settled," says the message, "but this is conditioned only that you immediately marry one another."

In order to settle the whole problem suitably the Viscount then suggests that the Countess marry M. Tibaudier and that she also give her servant Andree to his valet Jeannot for his wife.

"Yes, Monsieur Tibaudier," says the Countess, "I will marry you in order to enrage everyone."

"You do me a great honor," replies the counselor.

"And now that we are all properly enraged," says the Viscount, "let us proceed with the spectacle."

THE LEARNED WOMEN

THE LEARNED WOMEN

(LES FEMMES SAVANTES)

CHARACTERS IN THE PLAY

CHRYSALE: a good man of the middle class.

PHILAMINTE: wife of Chrysale.

ARMANDE, HENRIETTE: daughters of Chrysale and Philaminte.

ARISTE: brother of Chrysale.

BELISE: sister of Chrysale.

CLITANDRE: lover of Henriette.

TRISSOTIN: a wit.

VADIUS: a learned man.

MARTINE: servant of the household.

L'EPINE: a lackey.

JULIEN: valet of Vadius.

A NOTARY

The Scene is in Paris.

ACT I.

The play opens with a dialogue between Armande and her sister Henriette in which the former tries to persuade Henriette to take up the study of philosophy as her mother has done. Hearing that her sister is contemplating marriage, Armande disparages the idea and extols the satisfactions of philosophy. Henriette, however, compares such a life with that of domestic happiness which her lover Clitandre has offered her.

"I see nothing in the thought of having a husband, children, and a household that would wound my spirit and make me shudder," she says.

When, with these words, she refuses to obey her sister, Armande tells Henriette that Clitandre has made love to her. But this statement, prompted by Armande's jealousy of her sister, is immediately refuted when Clitandre himself appears upon the scene.

Henriette urges her lover to ask the consent of her mother and father for their marriage and Clitandre decides to hazard the adventure. Belise, the sister of Chrysale, who is Henriette's father, is asked to aid in the matter. But Belise believes that Clitandre is in love with her and thus witholds her cooperation.

ACT II.

Ariste, the brother of Chrysale, tells the latter that Clitandre is in love with Henriette and, acting as his ambassador to her parents, he urges Chrysale to give his consent to the marriage. Although Chrysale thinks well of the young man, and is persuaded by his brother to favor the suit, he is unfortunately under the shadow of his dominating wife.

During this conversation Belise enters and overhears what the two men are saying. She then tells them that they are mistaken in their ideas and asserts that she, and not

Henriette is the object of Clitandre's adoration. This statement very much astonishes, but does not convince, the two men.

Shortly thereafter, Philaminte, the wife of Chrysale, arrives on the scene. Her arrogant nature is shown by the fact that she is driving Martine, her servant, from the house, the sole crime of which she is guilty being that she does not use the most grammatical expressions while she is doing her work. Chrysale intercedes in her behalf and an altercation ensues between husband and wife over the point, in which the latter emerges victorious.

After this difficulty has been settled to the satisfaction of Philaminte, she informs Chrysale that she has chosen as the husband of Henriette a certain Monsieur Trissotin. This man is an adventurer, who has gotten into her good graces by exhibiting a small knowledge of Latin and a smaller knowledge of the art of poetry.

"I know that he does not have the honor of being in your good graces," says Philaminte to her husband, "but I am a better judge of his worth than you, and you are wasting your time to contest my decision."

Poor Chrysale is so overwhelmed by the information that he does not tell Philaminte of Clitandre's suit. Later, upon hearing of the affair, Ariste persuades his brother to declare his authority and become the real ruler of the household.

ACT III.

Having thus been prepared for an introduction to the "wise" Trissotin, we are given the opportunity of meeting this individual at closer range in the third act when he arrives at the home of Philaminte to read her a poem that he has just composed.

"It is a newly-born infant, Madame," says the poet, "and it is in your heart that I have come to deliver it."

The poem bears the title: "A Sonnet to the Princess Urania, upon her Fever." Henriette comes inadvertently into the room and wishes to withdraw, but her mother will not allow her to do so.

Trissotin then reads his poem and another, which he says impressively is entitled: "Upon a Carriage of Purple Color given to a Lady by her Friends." The ladies present, which include Armande and Belise, are extravagant in their praise of the decidedly commonplace and prosaic passages of which these poems are composed. During the reading, Vadius, a ·savant, is introduced to the ladies by Trissotin, but the two almost immediately come to hot words on account of the adverse criticism which Vadius makes of the poems. A violent verbal battle then ensues at the end of which Vadius is vanquished, who shouts as he departs: "I defy you in verse, prose, Greek, and Latin."

Shortly after this encounter, Philaminte informs Henriette that she is determined to have Trissotin as a son-in-law. This news greatly disturbs Henriette, but when Trissotin says: "I do not know what to say to you about my delight at this marriage with which you honor me," she replies tartly: "Not so fast, Monsieur, it is not yet consummated. Do not be in such a hurry."

Following this scene, Chrysale takes the opposide side by presenting his daughter to her lover Clitandre.

ACT IV.

Armande tries to poison her mother's ears with lies about Clitandre, but the latter, who arrives unannounced upon the scene, hears what is said about him and makes a splendid defense. In the course of this conversation he denounces his rival in no uncertain terms, but all of this has no influence upon either Philaminte or her daughter.

At this moment Trissotin arrives and a hot debate

ensues in which Clitandre attacks the sophistry of his rival. All that this accomplishes, however, is to have the entire group accuse Clitandre of being a champion of ignorance. While the issue is in doubt, a message is brought to Philaminte by Julien, the valet of Vadius, which denounces Trissotin as an impostor.

"Trissotin boasts, Madame, that he will espouse your daughter," says the message. "But I advise you that his philosophy has in view only your wealth, and you will do well not to conclude this marriage until you have seen the poem which I have composed against him."

But the only effect of this warning is to strengthen Philaminte's opinion of the adventurer and she determines to have the wedding celebrated that evening.

ACT V.

This act is devoted to the battle which Chrysale and his wife wage for the lordship of their house. The first scene is a conversation between Henriette and Trissotin in which the former accuses the latter of purely mercenary motives in his desire to marry her. He replies with a few hypocritical phrases calculated to express his genuine love for Henriette.

Chrysale arrives accompanied by Clitandre and Martine, the servant girl whom his wife has so summarily dismissed. He has always been fond of Martine and he determines to reinstate her in the household in spite of his wife's protest. This seems to be a good place to begin his battle for supremacy in his house.

Philaminte appears on the scene with Trissotin and a notary to prepare for the coming wedding. She is much surprised at her husband when he champions the cause of Clitandre, but she is unmoved in her determination and bids the notary prepare the necessary papers. A battle of words ensues and the poor notary is very much confused.

"Put down the name of Trissotin for my son-in-law," says Philaminte to the bewildered clerk.

"For my son-in-law write the name of Clitandre," says Chrysale.

"Two sons-in-law," mutters the notary. "Customarily that is too many."

Although Martine enters into the debate on the side of the supremacy of a husband in the rule of a household, the decision appears to be going against Chrysale. At this crucial moment Ariste arrives with two letters, one of which he gives to Philaminte and the other to his brother. These documents carry the bad news that both have lost their respective fortunes. This tale of misfortune immediately reveals the true characters of the rivals. Trissotin's interest in the marriage immediately wanes, but Clitandre turning to Philaminte, his detractor, says: "Madame, I attach myself to your destiny, and with myself I dare to offer you all that good fortune has given me."

After Trissotin has departed Ariste announces that the two messages were fakes, — artifices which he had contrived to reveal the true character of the impostor and the real worth of Clitandre. Her delusion having been thus dispelled from the eyes of Philaminte, she gives her consent to the marriage of Henriette and Clitandre and all ends happily.

Scene from The Imaginary Invalid.

THE IMAGINARY INVALID

THE IMAGINARY INVALID

(LE MALADE IMAGINAIRE)

CHARACTERS IN THE PLAY

ARGAN: the imaginary invalid.

BELINE: Argan's second wife.

ANGELIQUE: Argan's daughter; beloved by Cleante.

LOUISON: the small daughter of Argan and sister of Angelique.

BERALDE: Argan's brother.

CLEANTE: lover of Angelique.

MONSIEUR DIAFOIRUS: a physician.

THOMAS DIAFOIRUS: his son and lover of Angelique.

MONSIEUR PURGON: Argan's physician.

MONSIEUR FLEURANT: an apothecary.

MONSIEUR BONNEFOY: a notary.

TOINETTE: a servant.

The Scene is in Paris.

ACT I.

The play opens with a monologue by Argan, the imaginary invalid, in which he reviews the various prescriptions and the list of medicines, which he has used during his imaginary illness. Toinette, his servant, is not in sympathy with the ills of her master and takes delight in making sport of the physicians who are attending him.

"They make merry with your body," she says; "they have in you a good cow to milk. If I were you I would demand to know just what my illness is, which requires so many remedies."

"Be quiet," replies Argan irritably; "It is not your province to criticize the ordinances of medicine."

Argan then asks to see his daughter, Angelique, who has confided in Toinette that she has fallen in love with a young man, Cleante, whom she has just met. Her father, however, has chosen the son of a physician for his daughter's husband and breaks the news to her. In opening this conversation with Angelique, Argan recites all the virtues of the proposed suitor. Angelique believes that he is talking about Cleante, since the latter seems to possess these qualities, until her father says that he is studying medicine. Argan then reveals the name of the one whom he has chosen, namely, Thomas Diafoirus, the son of his physician, M. Diaphorus, and the nephew of his other physician, M. Purgon, who is also the brother-in-law of M. Diaphorus.

A stormy scene ensues in which Toinette defends Angelique against her father. She forces Argan to admit that he wants a physician for a son-in-law as a ready source of medicines for his malady; she elicits the further admission that the father also has his eyes open to business. Thomas will inherit his father's wealth and also that of his uncle, who has neither wife nor child, and who has an annual income of at least eight thousand livres. "What a lot of people he must have killed to be that rich!" says the lively Toinette.

Argan becomes so incensed at his daughter's opposition, that he threatens to place her in a convent unless she accedes to his wishes. Toinette appeals to the obdurate father to modify his demands, but to no avail. Finally, under the critical remarks of Toinette, Argan loses his temper and pursues her around the room with a stick. But the agile Toinette easily evades him and he finally sinks into a chair completely fatigued. "I can do no more," he moans. "Behold how it makes me die!"

Beline, the second wife of the sick man, appears on the scene and takes the part of her husband. She cajoles him with tender words and pretends to have a great affection for him.

Argan thinks that his wife cares so much about his health, that he decides to make his will in her favor, a thing which she has been working for. He also bestows upon her lavish gifts of money. Toinette, who sees through the conspiracy, tells Angelique that she will do all she can to help her.

ACT II.

Cleante, having been advised by Toinette of the state of affairs, appears on the scene under the guise of a substitute for Angelique's music teacher. While he is explaining the situation to Argan, Angelique appears and nearly reveals his identity in her surprise.

Monsieur Diafoirus and his son Thomas arrive at this time. Thomas is described as a great fool, recently out of school, who does everything badly and at the wrong time. He first makes a long address to Argan, extolling both the fine qualities of his own father and then the virtues of his prospective father-in-law. He then mistakes Angelique for Argan's wife and attempts to kiss her, an honor which Angelique respectfully avoids by bowing low. When finally informed of her identity, he addresses her with an extravagant speech. "As the statue of Memnon produces harmony when it is touched by the rays of the sun," he says, "so am I animated by sweet transports in the sun of your beauty. And as the heliotrope turns continually to the star of day, so also does my heart turn toward the resplendent stars of your eyes."

"Long live the college from which comes such a clever man!" says Toinette sarcastically. "If only Monsieur were as good a physician as he is an orator," says Cleante, "it would be a pleasure to be his patient."

M. Diafoirus in his turn praises his son. Although he confesses that the young man was slow in maturing, since he had not learned his letters by the time he was nine years old, he argues that this was, indeed, a very good thing. "Late trees bear the best fruit," he says. "One engraves with much more difficulty in marble than in sand."

Thomas then presents Angelique with a thesis which he has written. She refuses to accept it as being something she could not use, but Toinette urges her to take it. "We can use it to decorate our room," she says. The booby then concludes his remarks by inviting them to see a dissection. "Some lovers present a comedy for their beloved, but to invite them to a dissection is something much more flattering," says Toinette.

Argan then asks Cleante, the supposed music teacher, to have Angelique sing for them. The two act out a pastoral drama in which a shepherd and a shepherdess confess their love for each other, but are thwarted by the hardships imposed by an obdurate father. This greatly incenses Argan, who condemns the lovers in the play for their impudent comments about the father. ''We only wanted to divert you,'' says Cleante contritely, to which Argan replies: ''Such nonsense does not divert me.''

Beline arrives and is presented to the visitors, Thomas making his usual bumbling remarks on seeing her. Toinette tells Beline that she has been too late to hear him discourse on the virtues of fathers, the statue of Memnon, and the heliotrope.

Argan attempts to force Angelique to agree to her marriage with Thomas, in which he is aided by Beline, but she remains inflexible to all their arguments. Before Beline departs she informs Argan that, as she was passing Angelique's room, she saw her visiting with a young man. Since Argan's small daughter, Louison, was with them at the time, Beline suggests that Argan might gain some information by questioning her.

As soon as the guests have departed Argan acts on this advice and summons his small daughter. When he asks her to tell him about Angelique, she is evasive. Since she does not like the idea of spying on her sister, she refuses to give her father any information until he threatens her with a switching. She then reluctantly reveals the fact that the music teacher is merely Angelique's lover in disguise.

The act ends with a visit to Argan by his brother Beralde, a man endowed with a great deal of common sense. Argan reveals the state of affairs with Angelique and says that he shall send her to a convent within two days. Beralde counsels restraint. He then reveals that he has come to cure his brother of his illness by taking his mind off of his troubles. This he proposes to do by presenting before him a dance, interspersed with songs, which is given by a troupe of Egyptians and Moors. ''This should do you more good than all the prescriptions of Monsieur Purgon,'' he asserts.

ACT III.

Beralde, allying himself with the side of Angelique, attempts to bring his brother to his senses with regard both to his daughter and to his subservience to the physicians. In Beralde we hear Moliere expressing his own views of the medical art of his time in which, indeed, there was much to criticize. Beralde declares that all physicians are charlatans, and that one has the best chance of recovering from an illness if he refuses to take their medicines. Moreover, he says, if one does not escape death, at least he can die in peace.

Argan is horrified at these heresies. "Do you mean to say that the physicians know nothing?" he exclaims. "The fact is," replies Beralde, "they are well trained in the humanities; they speak excellent Latin; they know the Greek names of all the diseases; but as far as curing them, they know nothing at all." "But they surely know more than others," replies Argan. "That is what I have just said," answers Beralde; "they give words for reasons and promises for effects." Beralde then suggests that it will greatly benefit the health of his brother if he will go to see one of the comedies of Moliere. But of this suggestion Argan takes a dim view.

Monsieur Fleurant, an apothecary, arrives for his daily visit with the sick man. Beralde, however, dominates the scene, and, in the name of his brother, refuses to accept the nostrums. Fleurant leaves in a rage to report to Monsieur Purgon, leaving Argan in despair. "You have caused a great evil here," he says to his brother, to which Beralde replies that the only evil would be in taking the medicine. "Do you want to be a slave all your life to their remedies?"

Monsieur Purgon arrives in a rage. He will not let Argan explain that it is his brother's fault that the medicine was refused. He tells the invalid that he now abandons him to his many maladies, a list of which he recites. "That's good!" says Toinette, who is present at the interview.

As soon as Monsieur Purgon has departed, Toinette, dressed as a physician, arrives to see Argan. In this scene, by a clever exchange of dress, Toinette manages to play two parts, that of the maid and that of the physician. Argan expresses astonishment at the remarkable resemblance of the physician to Toinette, his maid, but he is completely fooled by the deception. Toinette claims to be a great traveling physician, who goes from place to place treating the sick. Having just arrived in the neighborhood, she has come to call upon Argan. Condemning in no uncertain terms the methods employed by other medical men, she at least partially reconciles Argan to his fate.

Toinette reappears as the maid and the argument is resumed about the love affair of Angelique, whom, Argan continues to avow, he is going to place in a convent. Argan then speaks of the great love his wife has for him. To confirm this, Toinette suggests that Argan pretend to be dead and hear what she has to say.

This the sick man does and is much disconcerted when the supposed loving Beline rejoices that she is now free. Argan comes to his senses immediately and his wife flees in dismay. Beralde then suggests that Argan try the same deception with his daughter. This experiment proves to be a complete reversal of the first and Argan is much moved by the show of affection which his daughter makes when she is advised of his death. This reconciles him to the thought of her marriage with Cleante.

The play ends with what we might call a medical ballet, in which a large group of physicians, surgeons, and apothecaries, flourishing the instruments of their trade, engage in a burlesque of their profession.

THE TRIALS OF A HARRIED HUSBAND

THE TRIALS OF A HARRIED HUSBAND

(LA JALOUSIE DU BARBOUILLE)

CHARACTERS IN THE PLAY

LE BARBOUILLE: husband of Angelique.

THE DOCTOR:

ANGELIQUE: daughter of Gorgibus.

VALERE: in love with Angelique.

CATHAU: Angelique's maid.

GORGIBUS: father of Angelique.

VILLEBREQUIN:

In this and the following play, the characters are listed under the words ACTEURS rather than PERSONNAGES.

The Scene is the entrance to Barbouille's house.

Le Barbouille is a stock character in Italian comedy. He usually appears with his face covered with flour.

As the play opens, Le Barbouille is complaining about the miserable life he leads with a wife whose main interests are high living and questionable associates rather than the care of her home and family. Unable to decide what to do about the situation, he calls to a Doctor who happens to be passing by and asks his advice. The Doctor, insulted because Le Barbouille does not remove his hat before addressing him, launches into a lengthy tirade in which he makes a ten-point claim to the title of doctor. Le Barbouille, who readily accepts the man's credentials and who merely wants an answer to his question, interrupts from time to time to try to present his problem. When he finally offers to pay the Doctor for his advice, the latter pretends to be insulted and walks away, with le Barbouille in close pursuit.

At this point Angelique arrives, accompanied by her lover and her maid. The conversation changes quickly from matters of love when they see Le Barbouille returning. Angelique, reprimanded by her husband for keeping company with another man, explains that this man has brought news of her brother's illness. Le Barbouille then turns on Cathau, accusing her of being a corrupting influence on his wife. The latter stops the discussion by suggesting that they just ignore him as being too drunk to know what he is saying.

Gorgibus, father of Angelique, arrives with Villebrequin and attempts to mediate the argument between his daughter and her husband. At this point the Doctor returns and offers his help in settling the dispute. When Gorgibus tries to explain the cause of their quarrel, the Doctor interrupts constantly with quotes from Socrates and others who have recommended the use of the fewest number of words necessary to say something. When Villebrequin tries to get into the conversation, the Doctor calls him an ignorant fool because he has not begun his speech in the proper manner. After inviting Angelique to present the case, the Doctor proceeds to interrupt her at every point, interjecting into his speech Latin quotations in order to show his erudition. Le Barbouille's attempt to get a word in merely brings on more insults. When the discussion finally turns into a shouting match, Le Barbouille fastens a rope to the Doctor's feet, trips him and then drags him from the scene, with the poor fellow still talking and counting on his fingers the ten reasons why he qualifies as a doctor.

Peace is finally restored, and all leave except Valere and a person named La Vallee, who for some unexplained reason is not listed among the cast of characters. The latter appears to have acted as a go-between in arranging a meeting between Valere and Angelique at the scene of a dance in a house nearby. By the time Angelique arrives, the dance is over. When she returns home, she finds that her husband, having become suspicious, has noted her absence and has locked her out of the house. Despite her protests of innocence and her declarations of love for him, he refuses at first to open the door. Angelique then threatens to kill herself with a knife she is carrying and points out that her parents will find her dead and will see that her husband is hanged for murder. Le Barbouille is not convinced, but when Angelique pretends to stab herself with the knife, he rushes down to check on her. In the darkness Angelique manages to get into the house and lock the door. Now she taunts her husband with the thought that when her parents arrive, they will at last realize that he is nothing but a no-good drunk who deserts his wife and children at night to waste his time and money drinking in the taverns.

At this point Gorgibus and Villebrequin arrive. Le Barbouille tries to defend himself against his father-in-law's accusations, and he refuses to apologize for his actions as suggested by Villebrequin. Gorgibus brings about a reconciliation between the two, just as the Doctor arrives on the scene dressed in nightclothes and complaining about the noise. When Villebrequin explains that everyone is now in agreement, the Doctor wants to read to the group a long chapter from Aristotle on the subject of love in the universe. The offer is declined, the Doctor bids them goodnight, in Latin of course, and the others go inside to have a bite to eat.

LE MÉDECIN MALGRÉ LUY

THE FLYING DOCTOR

THE FLYING DOCTOR

(LE MEDECIN VOLANT)

CHARACTERS IN THE PLAY

VALERE: in love with Lucile.

SABINE: cousin of Lucile.

SGANARELLE: valet of Valere.

GORGIBUS: father of Lucile.

GROS-RENE: valet of Gorgibus.

LUCILE: daughter of Gorgibus.

A LAWYER

Gorgibus wants his daughter Lucile to marry Ville-brequin, but Lucile is in love with Valere. In order to postpone the wedding, Lucile has feigned an illness, and she and her cousin Sabine conspire with Valere to find a doctor who will recommend that Lucile be lodged in a summer house, where she can see Valere at her pleasure and thwart her father's plans. Valere seeks out his faithful and clever valet, Sganarelle, who agrees to play the part of the doctor, for a price of course. Such a role will not be difficult since he can see to a patient's death as well as any doctor in the city. All he needs is some doctors' clothing and a little briefing on philosophy and mathematics so that he can quote Hippocrates and Galen.

As Gorgibus sends his valet Gros-Rene in search of a doctor, Sabine arrives with Sganarelle, who is presented to Gorgibus as the man who can cure Lucile's illness. With a bit of abracadabra, Sganarelle gains the confidence of Gorgibus, whereupon he asks for a sample of urine from the patient. Sabine returns shortly with a liquid sample which Sganarelle promptly swallows, to the surprise and consternation of Gorgibus. Sganarelle explains that, unlike other doctors who are content to look at urine samples, he is able to determine causes and cures for ailments by tasting the liquid.

Sganarelle now asks to see the patient, for whom he prescribes fresh country air. As they are about to leave to see whether the country house will be satisfactory, Gorgibus' lawyer arrives to offer his assistance. Declaring that he is flattered to make the acquaintance of such a learned man, he takes leave shortly, and Sganarelle accepts, reluctantly of course, an offer of some money from Gorgibus. As the latter enters his house, Valere comes in search of Sganarelle, who now returns dressed as a valet. As they discuss how well things are going, Gorgibus returns and Sganarelle is put to the test of their little scheme. He p r e t e n d s to be the poor unfortunate twin brother of a famous doctor believed to have arrived in town recently, and with whom he is at odds. Gorgibus promises to bring the two brothers together. Sganarelle expresses his thanks, takes leave, and returns immedi- ately in his doctors' dress. Gorgibus tells him of having seen his poor brother recently, whereupon Sganarelle expresses first contempt, then forgiveness, for the drunk- en derelict.

Gorgibus goes in search of the poor brother, and Sgan- arelle, having changed into his valet garb, is talking with Valere when they see Gorgibus returning. Valere escapes, unseen by Gorgibus, who thinks he has found the poor brother.

The rest of the play is a series of similar situations from which the clever valet always escapes, in spite of the suspicions aroused in Gros-Rene and finally in Gorgibus himself. Sganarelle finds himself entering and leaving by windows as his pursuers attempt to determine whether he is really one person or two. He finds it necessary on oc- casion to fake arguments between the two brothers when Gorgibus succeeds in getting "both" of them into the house at the same time. At Gros-Rene's insistence, Gor- gibus orders the two brothers to appear together at a window. Sganarelle pretends to be embracing the other brother by embracing his hat and ruffs, and Gorgibus is satisfied. Sganarelle then comes out in doctors' dress and gives the house key to Gorgibus, saying that he does not wish to be seen in the company of his brother and that Gorgibus may let him out when he wishes. He then pre- tends to leave but returns quickly after ridding himself of the doctors' coat and enters the house through a win- dow. Gorgibus goes to the house and returns immediately with Sganarelle in his valet dress.

Meanwhile, Gros-Rene has discovered the robe discarded by Sganarelle, and the game is over. Sganarelle confesses his part in the scheme but assures Gorgibus that he will be pleased, since Valere is both noble and wealthy. The lovers appear, and Gorgibus proposes a celebration and a toast to the health of the entire company.

LE MALADE IMAGINAIRE.

Scene from The Critique of the School for Wives.

THE CRITIQUE OF THE SCHOOL FOR WIVES

THE CRITIQUE OF THE SCHOOL FOR WIVES

(LA CRITIQUE DE L'ECOLE DES FEMMES)

CHARACTERS IN THE PLAY

URANIE

ELISE

CLIMENE

GALOPIN: lackey.

THE MARQUIS

DORANTE, or THE CHEVALIER:

LYSIDAS: poet.

The Scene is Uranie's drawing room, in Paris.

The play opens with Uranie and Elise discussing the kinds of people that frequent the former's salon. Elise cannot understand how Uranie can endure all these people. Uranie explains that she enjoys those who are reasonable and that those who are characters amuse her. Conversation then turns to a certain Marquis, an insufferable bore, whose penchant for punning is very annoying to Elise. At this moment Galopin announces the arrival of Climene. Elise would have preferred not to see this person, but Galopin has already told her that Madame is in. While awaiting the new arrival, Elise describes her in vivid terms as a stupid animal, the most affected of the *precieuses*. She then relates the story of an occasion when Climene invited a famous wit to dine with her, expecting that he would entertain her and her guests. To the chagrin of the hostess, the so-called wit, probably Moliere himself, failed to cooperate and remained strangely silent during the entire evening.

Climene arrives, exhausted, weak and ill. She has just come from the Palais-Royal, where she witnessed a presentation of *The School for Wives*. Uranie explains that she and Elise saw the play two days before and that they both enjoyed it and returned home hale and hearty. While Elise finds Climene's criticism of specific points in the play charming, elegant and eloquent, Uranie defends the play itself, including accusations of indecency, dirt and filth, particularly in the scene where Arnolphe is trying to find out whether a young man has "taken something" from Agnes. Uranie points out that not a dirty word has been spoken by Agnes and that anyone who finds the scene objectionable must be inserting his own dirty thoughts into it.

At this moment the Marquis arrives, and Galopin, having been chastised previously for letting Climene in, tries to prevent the new arrival from entering. Uranie comes to the latter's rescue and welcomes him into her presence. The Marquis has just come from the theater, where he was roughed up trying to reach his seat on the stage. Just then Dorante, who has been expected for supper, arrives, and the discussion of the play resumes. Dorante defends the play, which the Marquis finds "detestable because it is detestable." When asked why the play is detestable, the Marquis doesn't really know because he didn't bother to listen. The roars of laughter from the pit were enough to convince him that the play was bad. Dorante then defends the opinion of the pit, insisting that those able to afford better seats are not necessarily better judges of the worth of a play and that, in fact, persons of rank seem to be wrong more often than right in their opinions. Even clever persons often refuse to agree with a proper judgment because they want the glory of making the decisions. As for elegant ladies who find the play distasteful, Dorante explains that they are substituting prudery for the youth and beauty which they no longer have, and that they have no right to be scandalized by what they have seen.

At this moment Lysidas, a poet and author, arrives. He has just come from a reading of his most recent play at the home of the Marquise, and the lengthy praise of his work has detained him. When asked to comment on Moliere's play, Lysidas begs off at first, not wishing to criticize the work of a fellow-author. When he finally asks whether the play is not indeed the finest in the world, his sincerity is questioned by Dorante, who then tries to get him to say that the play is a wretched piece of work. Lysidas appears to weaken a bit, at which point all except Uranie turn on Dorante. Uranie, speaking in general terms, defends the play without offending Climene, who finds in it a disagreeable satire against women. When she objects to the word animals being applied to women, Uranie shows that this is not bad, since it is said by a ridiculous character. Lysidas then laments the neglect of serious drama in Paris. This leads to a defense of comedy by both Uranie and Dorante. The latter explains that it requires little imagination to write a tragedy, whereas a comedy must be a painting from nature, in order that people may recognize themselves. This is doubly difficult because it must also be amusing. When Climene, the Marquis and Lysidas insist that they found nothing witty in the play, Dorante reminds them that that was not the opinion of the Court, which he hastens to declare to be the final judge of a play's worth and not a bad one at that.

Discussion now turns to the question of whether the play is good, from a technical point of view. Lysidas insists that it violates the rules of art, particularly those of Aristotle and Horace, but Dorante counters with the suggestion that the first rule is to please. Uranie observes that she has noticed that those who know the rules best write the poorest comedies. Dorante then defends the play against accusations of violations of the "rules." The lack of action is explained in that the accounts themselves are in effect actions. The "children through the ear" remark of Agnes is defended as a means of showing the absurdity of Arnolphe, who considers such a trivial remark as the funniest thing in the world.

Arnolphe's giving money to his rival is likewise adequately defended by Dorante, as are the lengthy scenes with Alain and Georgette and Arnolphe's moral speech, or sermon, which some found irreverent. As for the love scene near the end of the play, considered by some to be too exaggerated, Dorante wonders whether even the most serious men of breeding don't, on similar occasions, sometimes do things just as foolish. At this point Uranie observes that so many funny things have happened in this discussion that Moliere should be apprised of them so

that he can make them into a play. The trouble would be
finding an ending for a story which has no marriage or
recognition. When Galopin comes to announce that supper
is on the table, Dorante finds this the most natural ending
for the story, and Uranie suggests that the play terminate
here.

THE VERSAILLES IMPROMPTU

THE VERSAILLES IMPROMPTU

(L'IMPROMPTU DE VERSAILLES)

CHARACTERS IN THE PLAY

MOLIERE: a ridiculous marquis.

BRECOURT: a man of quality.

LA GRANGE: a ridiculous marquis.

DU CROISY: a poet.

LA THORILLIERE: a marquis and a bore.

BEJART: a busybody.

MLLE. DU PARC: a ceremonious marquise.

MLLE. DE BRIE: a prudent coquette.

MLLE. MOLIERE: a satirical wit.

MLLE. DU CROISY: a mealymouthed pest.

MLLE. HERVE: a *precieuse* ladies' maid.

FOUR BUSYBODIES

The description of the parts are those of the characters in the play-within-a-play. The designations are not very exact and probably were not written by Moliere. The characters are members of Moliere's company, and the play brings out not only the problems encountered by such a company and its director, but also something of the personality of the members as seen by Moliere.

The Scene is the royal theater at Versailles.

This work is in the nature of a play-within-a-play in which Moliere is rehearsing his company in a piece which he has written very hurriedly, on orders of the king, to be presented as an answer to critics of his *School for Wives*.

As the play opens, Moliere calls all his actors one at a time, by name, explains that they have two hours before the king's arrival, and orders a rehearsal of the play which they are to present. All the actors protest that they have not had time to learn their parts, and they fear that they will not do well. Mlle. Bejart and Mlle. de Brie think that Moliere should not have risked his reputation by attempting to put on the play with so little time to prepare, but Moliere says that one must do as the king bids. To a comment by Mlle. Moliere, he replies, "Be quiet, wife, you're a fool," to which his wife of twenty months replies that marriage changes people and that he would not have said that to her a year and a half before.

Mlle. Bejart asks Moliere why he did not do, instead, a thing which he had discussed with some of the company. In it he had planned to parody the actors of the Hotel de Bourgogne who had appeared in a play called *The Portrait of the Painter,* in which Moliere and his *School for Wives* had been lampooned. Moliere explains that he was not sure that he could have done all the characters well, since he had not studied them sufficiently and had seen the play only once. At Mlle. de Brie's prodding, Moliere reluctantly demonstrates what he had had in mind, imitating five of the rival actors and actresses in speeches taken from tragedies by Corneille. In each case he recites the lines first in a natural way, then in the grandiloquent style used by the rival company, asking after each demonstration whether the natural style is not better.

The rehearsal must get on. After explaining that the marquis has now replaced the clownish servant as the butt of comedy, Moliere discusses with each actor the part he is to play and how he should play it. Mlle. du Parc, the least affected of the actresses of the company, has the part of a ceremonious marquise. She will do well, not only because she is a good actress, but also because she has just done an excellent job in a similar role as Climene in the *Critique*. Du Croisy is the dramatic poet, a role he played in the *Critique* as Lysidas. Brecourt will play a well-bred courtier, the same role he had as Dorante in the *Critique*, Mlle. Bejart will portray a prude, Mlle. de Brie a coquette for whom appearance is everything, while Mlle. Moliere will play the same character she did in the *Critique*, that of Elise. The remainder of the parts are assigned, and the rehearsal is about to begin when La Thorilliere, one of those ridiculous marquises referred to by Moliere, comes on the scene and delays the proceedings by asking a lot of silly questions and making a general nuisance of himself. Moliere finally gets rid of him by explaining that the ladies prefer not to have visitors during a rehearsal.

Moliere and La Grange have the first scene. Each is a ridiculous marquis, and one of the first questions to be answered is which of the two is the marquis impersonated in the *Critique*. Each wagers that it is the other, and they call on Brecourt to be the judge. Brecourt explains that neither of them can be the one impersonated, since Moliere does not depict individuals but rather characters, which he invents and dresses up to entertain the spectators. If a character created by Moliere corresponds to someone in society, that should not be surprising, since it is the business of comedy to represent in general all the defects of men. When Moliere the marquis suggests that Moliere the writer may have run out of subjects and will find no more material for his plays, Moliere the director rehearses Brecourt in a lengthy reply, in which he lists the many untouched areas still available. At this point Mlle. du Parc and Mlle. Moliere arrive for their part, which is virtually a reenactment of the roles played by the two in the *Critique,* as the younger woman flatters the ceremonious marquise.

In the next scene Du Croisy, as Lysidas the poet, arrives with the news that a play written against Moliere is to be put on by the actors of the Hotel de Bourgogne. Although all the enemies of Moliere have had a part in painting this portrait of him, they have purposely chosen an author with no reputation to put his name to the work. The other members of the cast then join in criticism of Moliere as they repeat the charges that have been made by his enemies during the quarrel over the *School for Wives.* Mlle. Moliere observes that Moliere deserves this public attack for having written plays that all Paris goes to see, and in which he portrays people so well that everyone recognizes himself. He should write as Lysidas does and he would avoid all these p r o b l e m s, including the crowds and the income from his plays. When Moliere the marquis suggests that with everyone against him, Moliere the writer will have to go into hiding, Brecourt insists that on the contrary, Moliere will sit on the stage and laugh with the others at the portrait they have made of him. Furthermore, he will laugh the loudest because the only good parts are the ideas taken from Moliere. To the suggestion that Moliere should reply further to his critics, Brecourt insists that the best answer he can make is to write another successful play which will take away their audiences.

At this point Mlle. Bejart interrupts the rehearsal to express her opinion that Moliere should again attack his critics, whereupon Moliere answers that he would only be helping his enemies to make money, which is what they want. He insists further that his only crime has been that of being successful in pleasing those he wants to please, and that when people attack a successful play, they are attacking the judgment of those who have approved it rather than the art of the one who wrote it. As for Boursault, the insignificant author of the *Portrait,* Moliere will not help him by keeping him in the limelight. Instead he will be on with his work, which the critics may tear apart and from which they may derive some profit. He asks only that they stop attacking him on personal matters, such as his religion and his married life.

When Mlle. Bejart tries to pursue the matter further, Moliere insists that they stop wasting time making speeches and get on with the rehearsal. While all are protesting that they cannot possibly put the show together in the time left to them, Bejart arrives to announce that the king is waiting for them to begin. Moliere asks for a little more time. There follows a succession of busybodies heckling Moliere and trying to get the show started. The situation is saved when Bejart returns to report that the king realizes the plight they are in and will allow them to postpone this new play, provided they will entertain him with another of their choosing.

BIBLIOGRAPHY

A complete bibliography of Molière would be inappropriate to a work of this nature. The following booklist was used by the editors and may be helpful in the further study of Molière's life and works.

EDITIONS:

Editions Garnier Frères. Paris, 1962. Published in two volumes as *Oeuvres complètes de Molière*, with a preface by Robert Jouanny, and in virtually identical form as *Théâtre complet de Molière*, in the collection "Classiques Garnier." The bibliography contained in this work lists fourteen additional editions of complete works of Molière, including that of La Grange and Vinot, published in 1682.

Théâtre complet de Molière. Paris, Hachette. Five volumes.

Rat, Maurice, *Théâtre Choisi de Molière*. Paris, Garnier Frères. (No publication date shown).

Turgeon and Gilligan, *The Principal Comedies of Molière*. New York, The MacMillan Company, 1947.

BIOGRAPHY AND CRITICISM:

Bray, René, *Molière, Homme de Théâtre*. Mercure de France, 1954.

Chapman, Percy A. *The Spirit of Molière*. New York, Russell and Russell, Inc., 1965.

Encyclopaedia Britannica, 11th Edition.

Encyclopaedia Britannica, Current Edition.

Fernández, Ramón, *Molière, the Man Seen through the Plays*. A translation by Wilson Follett of *La Vie de Molière*. New York, Hill and Wang, Inc., 1960.

Gossman, Lionel, *Men and Masks, a Study of Molière*. Baltimore, The Johns Hopkins Press, 1963.

Grimarest, *Vie de Monsieur de Molière*. Reprint in 1150 copies of the text of the original work published in Paris in 1705. Paris, La Renaissance du Livre, 1930.

Hubert, J. D., *Molière and the Comedy of Intellect*. Berkeley, University of California Press, 1962.

Lancaster, Henry C., *A History of French Dramatic Literature in the Seventeenth Century*. New York, Gordian Press, Inc., 1966.

Larroumet, Gustave, *La Comédie de Molière, l'auteur et le milieu*. Paris, Hachette, 1887.

Lewis, D. B. Wyndham, *Molière: the Comic Mask*. New York, Coward-McCann, Inc., 1959.

Matthews, Brander, *Molière, his Life and his Works*. New York, Scribners, 1916.

TRANSLATIONS:

Eight Plays by Molière. New York, The Modern Library, 1957. Introduction by Morris Bishop.

Molière's Comedies. New York, Dutton, 1929. Two Volumes, with Introduction by F. C. Green.

Plays by Molière. New York, Random House, 1950. Introduction by Francis Fergusson.

Six Prose Comedies of Molière. London, Oxford University Press, 1956. Translated by George Graveley.

TRANSLATIONS:

Tartuffe and Other Plays by Molière. New York. The New American Library, Inc., 1967. Translation and Introduction by Donald E. Frame.

The Works of Molière. New York, Benjamin Blom, Inc., 1967. Six volumes. Translation and biography of Molière by John Ozell. First published in London in 1714.